A T[illegible]

Prairie Life

Recipes
Remedies
Reminiscings

by Loaun
Werner
Vaad

Published by:
Loaun Werner Vaad
HC 69, Box 210
Chamberlain, SD 57325
605-734-5135

Library Of Congress Catalog Number:
96-90357

ISBN: 0-9652586-3-7

Vol. 1, First and Second Printings
at Register-Lakota Printing, Chamberlain, SD

Other books available:
The Best Little Cookbook In The West

Ordering information is provided in back of book.

Join me on the prairie. We will savor recipes old and new. Not all are original, but all are favorites; created and collected by people of the northern plains. Meet interesting people, discover unforgettable places, and enjoy remedies and recollections of prairie life in times gone by.

As lifestyles change so do cooking habits; we find ourselves reading recipes and cookbooks more than using them! Included in this book are stories, writings and favorite sayings in addition to the recipes. This isn't just a cookbook; it is the people of the prairies sharing "A Taste of Prairie Life".

Read, Taste and Enjoy,
Loaun

ARABIAN PROVERB

A true friend is one to whom
one may pour out all of the
contents of one's heart,
chaff and grain together,
knowing that the gentlest of hands
will take and sift it,
keep what is worth keeping
and, with the breath of kindness,
blow the rest away.

Prairie winds change quickly from calming breezes to gale-force tempests. Temperatures can vary in excess of 50 degrees from one day to the next, as spring-like weather suddenly switches to a roaring blizzard. And yet the northern plains remain beautiful and serene much like its peoples; hearty but gentle, unchanged by the sometimes harsh conditions with which they live.

In the center of this land of rolling hills, Missouri River breaks, buffalo grass and pollution free skies, Loaun Werner was born and raised. She returned to make the prairies her home with her husband, Jerry Vaad, and children Tracy and Travis.

Jerry and Loaun have a small ranch in addition to his work in the recreation department at St. Joseph's Indian School and her framing and art business. Tracy presently owns and operates a gift shop business plus the decorative pheasant feather wreath business started by Loaun. Travis has worked as a counselor and currently hails from Nashville, Tennessee where he is pursuing a songwriting career.

Pasqueflower

Other names: crocus, wild crocus, lion's beard, prairie anemone, windflower, blue tulip, prairiesmoke, easterflower, prairie crocus, April fool, badger, easter plant, gosling, hartshorn, rock lily

Latin names: Anemone patens, Pulsatilla ludoviciana
Anemone is derived from Greek meaning wind, patens is from Latin meaning spreading.

Family: Buttercup (Ranunculaceae) or crowfoot

The pasque arises with the first spring breeze and is the first on the prairies in the spring. As one of the earliest of flowers on the Dakota landscape, they have thrived on the dry soil of the prairie lands. Hal Borland has written, "Of all the early wildflowers these are the bravest..." These handsome harbingers of spring also have religious significance being called easterflowers. They often bloom during the Easter (Paschal, hence pasque) or Passover season. The Pasque has been used for medicinal purposes by Native Americans and in Europe.

The pasqueflower is very hardy. Usually a single plant, the outer parts of the flower, which look like petals, are actually sepals and vary from white to deep purple. The color variance is thought to reflect life processes but may also be genetic. The flowers mature to a fluffy seed pod, hence several of its other names.

DEDICATION

This book is dedicated to Hal Werner. His photo of the pasque-flower, used on the cover, is a wonderful asset to my cookbook. He has been an enthusiastic consultant as well as brother extraordinaire.

PRAIRIE WISDOM

Discovering the joy of a clear spring puddle, our toddler emitted exclamations of excitement as the water soaked through his orthopedic shoes to the awaiting feet. As my chiding echoed around the ranch yard, Grampa, who had come for a visit, grinned and said, "Life is tough for little boys and old men." This was only one of Grampa's numerous wise sayings that I would come to value.

Grampa's wisdom was not something he flaunted; in fact, he would not even have considered anything he shared to have an impact past a fleeting comment. The truth is that this man with six years of formal education exemplified values, morals, and work ethic that were the foundation for a living legacy.

My husband's relationship with Dad allowed me to understand how unique and effective his theories could be. Approaching the courting age, our daughter soon determined that our ideas were not parallel with hers. It was during one of these discussions that my husband Jim said, "Gloria, your dad's philosophy was sound." When I was growing up, we were not allowed to go to a dance or other social events with the girls. If we left the house with an escort of Dad's approval, he would know that would be the person who would bring us home (or it better be). Leaving the house alone and meeting up with a group in town would leave a possible match unknown to my dad. Make sense? It did to me now as I was a parent; as a teenager I had no understanding of it.

It took years of experience and maturity for me to appreciate Dad's statement, "The less you say, the better off you are." As I invaded the classroom as a novice teacher of high school and middle school students, it was these words of wisdom that empowered me with the aura of the unknown, a tool for leaving students cautious in their approaches to mischief. Faced with a conversation that could entrap you in gossip? Approached by an irate colleague who targets you as a release for his or her anger? Involved in a business enterprise that requires some quiet reflection instead of rash judgment? Consider these words: The less you say, the better off you are.

Approaching his golden years, Dad was talking about investing in insurance for covering the cost of care in a retirement home. It was now that I knew I had a wise comment. "Dad, do you really think that is necessary? You have six living children. If you depleted your funds, each of the kids could assist by paying for two months." With a coy smile Dad spoke quietly and gently, "It is easier for one dad to take care of six kids than it is for six kids to take care of one dad."

Even though the grasses bend with storms and wind, the prairie perseveres the elements of challenge. Before our family shared Dad and Grampa with the Lord, he endured the challenge of cancer. Like the prairie he persevered. God was his fortress and strength. His legacy lives in the words of wisdom he shared.

===

Gloria Schaefer is the owner of Dynamics for Excellence headquartered north of Kennebec, South Dakota. She researches and develops selected presentations for any organization or business. Her enthusiastic, professional style is shared through messages of inspiration, motivation, education, and patriotism. Gloria taught 23 years and continues to ranch with her husband Jim. To enhance your next meeting, call 605-869-2357.

RECIPE FOR A HAPPY HOME

1 cup honesty
1 cup congeniality
2 cups of plenty
3 cups respect
4 cups of love

Stir honesty to a smooth mixture. Add four portions of love, well beaten. Moisten with one cup of congeniality. Stir slowly the three cups of respect. Season with the fruit of the spirit. Add a dash of the spice of unselfishness and a pinch of the salt of individuality. Lighten with loaves of consistency. Bake in a quick oven.

TABLE OF CONTENTS

DAKOTA

My thoughts wander to the mountains
And then come back to the plain
My heart goes out to the seashore
And then it comes back again

With the hills and plains together
Where the rivers wind their way
I long to be in Dakota
Ere the passing of this day

Take me back to old Dakota
Where the sky and earth seem blended
Back to that glorious country
Where every heartache is mended

I have wandered far over the ocean
I have visited foreign lands
But I long for old Dakota
More than for desert sands

You may go to every large city
Across this large earth you may roam
But you'll not find a place sweeter
Than my old Dakota home

And when my roaming is over
Oh I long for that golden West
So take me back to Dakota
Where I can have Home and Rest

This poem was written by my mother,
Edith Harless Werner, in 1925
when she was 12 years old.

NOTES:

CAN SIZES

Picnic size can - 1 1/4 cups
No. 300 size can - 1 3/4 cups
No. 1 Tall size can - 2 cups
No. 303 size can - 2 cups
No. 2 size can - 2 1/2 cups
No. 2 1/2 size can - 3 1/2 cups
No. 3 size can - 4 cups
No. 10 size can - 12 cups

MEASUREMENTS

4 tablespoons - 1/4 cup
5 1/2 tablespoons - 1/3 cup
8 tablespoons - 1/2 cup
3 teaspoon - 1 tablespoon
16 tablespoons - 1 cup
2 cups - 1 pint
2 pints - 1 quart
8 ounces - 1 cup
16 ounces - 1 pound
4 quarts liquid - 1 gallon
8 quarts solid - 1 peck
4 pecks - bushel
1 gallon - 128 ounces
1 quart - 32 ounces
1 pint - 16 ounces
1 cup - 8 ounces
1 teaspoon - 1/8 ounce
1 dash - 3 drops

OVEN TEMPERATURES

Slow temperature - 300 degrees
Slow moderate temperature - 325 degrees
Moderate temperature - 350 degrees
Quick moderate temperature - 375 degrees
Moderate hot temperature - 400 degrees
Hot temperature - 425 degrees
Very hot temperature - 475 degrees

OVEN BAKING CHART

These are typical baking times and usually will work if your recipe doesn't give the baking temperatures and times.

Biscuits - 450 for 12-15 minutes
Muffins - 400-425 for 20-25 minutes
Quick breads - 350 for 40-60 minutes
Yeast breads - 375-400 for 45-60 minutes
Yeast rolls - 400 for 25-20 minutes
Cupcakes - 375 for 20-25 minutes
Layer cakes - 350-375 for 25-35 minutes
Drop or rolled cookies 350-375 for 8-12 minutes
Bar cookies - 350 for 25-30 minutes
Two crust pies - 450 for 10 minutes,
350 for 40 minutes

ABBREVIATIONS FOR STATES

Alabama	AL
Alaska	AK
Arizona	AZ
Arkansas	AR
California	CA
Colorado	CO
Connecticut	CT
Delaware	DE
District of Columbia	DC
Florida	FL
Georgia	GA
Guam	GM
Hawaii	HI
Idaho	ID
Illinois	IL
Indiana	IN
Iowa	IA
Kansas	KS
Kentucky	KY
Louisiana	LA
Maine	ME
Maryland	MD
Massachusetts	MA
Michigan	MI
Minnesota	MN
Mississippi	MS
Missouri	MO
Montana	MT
Nebraska	NE
Nevada	NV
New Hampshire	NH
New Jersey	NJ
New Mexico	NM
New York	NY
North Carolina	NC
North Dakota	ND
Ohio	OH
Oklahoma	OK
Oregon	OR
Pennsylvania	PA
Puerto Rico	PR
Rhode Island	RI
South Carolina	SC
South Dakota	SD
Tennessee	TN
Texas	TX
Utah	UT
Vermont	VT
Virginia	VA
Virgin Islands	VI
Washington	WA
West Virginia	WV
Wisconsin	WI
Wyoming	WY

ANNIVERSARY GIFT LIST

First	Paper
Second	Cotton
Third	Glass
Fourth	Flowers
Fifth	Wood
Sixth	Candy
Seventh	Wool
Eighth	Linen
Ninth	Leather
Tenth	Tin
Eleventh	Steel
Twelfth	Silk
Thirteenth	Lace
Fourteenth	Ivory
Fifteenth	Crystal
Twentieth	Pearl
Twenty fifth	Silver
Thirtieth	Pearl
Thirty fifth	Coral
Fortieth	Ruby
Forty fifth	Sapphire
Fiftieth	Gold
Seventy fifth	Diamond

BIRTHSTONES

January	Garnet
February	Amethyst
March	Aquamarine
April	Diamond
May	Emerald
June	Pearl
July	Ruby
August	Sardonyx
September	Sapphire
October	Opal
November	Topaz
December	Turquoise

My Mother and my Uncle Hal have always enjoyed reciting old poetry and excerpts from plays that they learned at the Hamill school. You are getting a taste of that part of my prairie life!

Smile
awhile, And while you
smile,
Another **smiles**, and soon
There's miles and miles of
smiles,
And life's worth while
Because you
smile.

anon

NOTES:

Meat and Taters

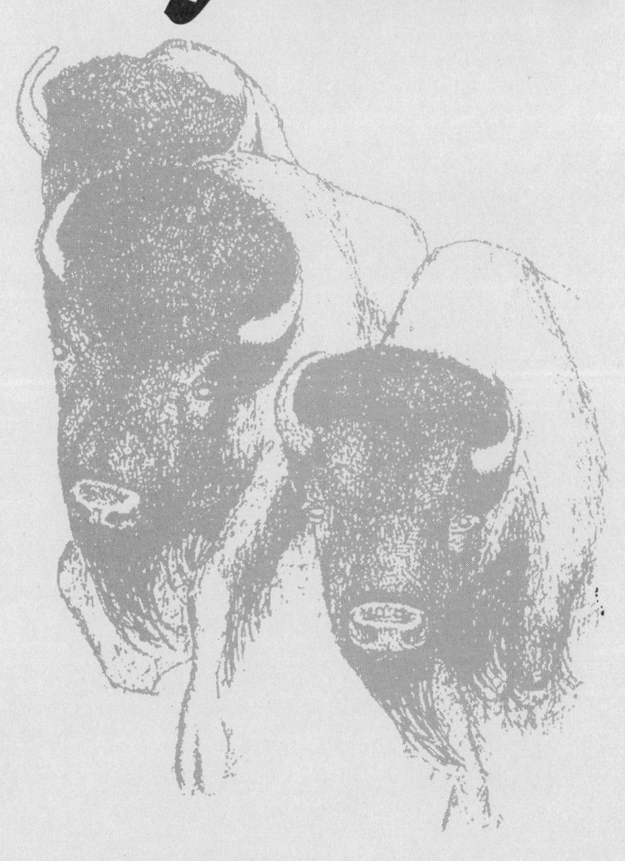

Pheasant In Cream
Easy Company Chicken
Cola Roast Beef
Yorkshire Pudding
All Day Stew
Wax Beans Supreme
Barbecued Meatballs
Country Lamb Casserole
Chicken 'n Rice Pan
"Batter Up" Fish
Oven Buffalo Stroganoff
Barbecued Hamburger for 20
Mighty Easy Meat Loaf
Rattlesnake Steaks
Tuna Rice Patties
Pheasant Sausage
Ham and Noodle Casserole
Prairie Oysters
"Dill"icious Burger Bake
Hot Dog and Potato Skillet
Medicine Creek Egg Scramble
Venison and Sausage Meatballs
Pineappled Pork
Corn Chowder
Sour Cream Beef Stew
Prairie Pasta
Salmon Casserole
BLT Soup
Roux
A Dozen Sloppy Joes
Cold Tater Bake
Clam Chowder
Vegetable Soup
Taco Soup
Travis's Mexican Omelette
Roast Beef and Dressing
Tracy's Spaghetti Sauce
Wild Rice Soup
Old Fashioned Strudels
Grilled Walleye with Grilled Corn
Donna's Deviled Beef Stew
Microwave Meat Loaf
Steak Bistechine
Walleye Fish Fritters

PHEASANT IN CREAM

4 pheasant breasts, skinned and boned
Flour, seasoned with salt and pepper
Butter and cooking oil
1/2 cup diced onion
1/2 cup diced celery
1 cup sliced fresh mushrooms
1 cup cream of mushroom soup
1 cup whipping cream
1/2 cup white wine

Dust pheasant breasts in seasoned flour. Saute in half butter and half oil until lightly browned. Place in casserole dish. Make sauce by sauteing the onion, celery and mushrooms in butter. Add the soup, cream and wine. Blend together and pour over the pheasant. Bake covered in 300 degree oven for 2 hours. Serve with wild rice and sliced apples. Enjoy!

The Pheasant In Cream recipe was shared with us by the ***Thunderstik Lodge***, located a few minutes from Chamberlain, South Dakota. Thunderstik provides five-star accommodations and premier customer service for a one of a kind hunting experience. In addition to pheasant hunting, they offer some of the best duck and goose hunts. And after the hunt you'll be able to unwind in the Sundowner Room which provides a relaxing atmosphere and a breathtaking view of the Missouri River.

EASY COMPANY CHICKEN

6 pieces of chicken
1 pound bag California blend frozen vegetables
1 package dry chicken gravy mix
1/2 teaspoon seasoning salt
1/2 cup orange juice concentrate*

Place chicken in baking dish. Pour frozen, uncooked vegetables over the chicken and sprinkle with dry gravy mix and seasoning salt. Pour orange juice over top. Cover dish and bake at 350 degrees about 1 hour. Remove cover to allow chicken to brown during last 15 minutes of baking or turn on broiling unit until it browns nicely. Serve with rice.

*Note: use orange juice instead of concentrate if you would like a milder orange flavor.

Flour and salt mixed into vinegar will shine your copper ware.

COLA ROAST BEEF

This takes several hours cooking time but a minimum of preparation and no watching.

3 to 4 pound pot or chuck roast
1 1/2 cups catsup
1 can cola

Place roast in pan. Pour catsup over meat; then pour cola over catsup. Cover and cook at 325 degrees for 3 to 4 hours.

Haven't you always wanted to try Yorkshire Pudding? Couple it with this easy Cola Roast, and you'll have the time to make it. Find the recipe on page 26.

YORKSHIRE PUDDING

2 eggs, beaten well
1 cup milk
1 cup flour
1 teaspoon salt
Roast drippings or fat, 1/3 cup will do

Heat roast drippings in a rectangular baking dish at 450 degrees while mixing up pudding. Add milk to eggs and carefully stir in dry ingredients. Beat to remove any lumps. Pour into the heated dish. Reduce heat to 350 degrees and bake approximately 30 minutes. Serve cut in slices and covered with gravy.

ALL DAY STEW

1 1/2 pounds stew meat, cubed
5 carrots
4 stalks celery
1 medium onion
1 large potato
1 cup fine bread crumbs
3 tablespoons quick tapioca
15 ounce can tomatoes
Salt and pepper

Chop vegetables. Place all items in a dutch oven. Place in a 300 degree oven for 6 to 9 hours. This recipe should serve six.

Ground cloves sprinkled on their paths may convince little red ants to stay away. A sprinkling of red pepper or a line of petroleum jelly may also work.

WAX BEANS SUPREME

1 can wax beans
1 can Vienna sausages
Cheese sauce*
1 cup cheese flavored crackers

Arrange partially drained wax beans in casserole dish. Pour on your favorite cheese sauce or a cheese soup. Place Vienna sausage slices on top and cover with the crushed cheese crackers. Bake 25 minutes at 400 degrees.

* There is a cheese sauce recipe included in the Medicine Creek Egg Scramble recipe.

If watching your fat intake, you may be able to eat the meats you like in moderate portions if you remember to "Trim And Skim To Make It Slim", but check with your doctor if you have a health problem!

BARBECUED MEATBALLS

1 1/2 pounds hamburger
3 tablespoons milk
1 tablespoon onion, diced
1 egg
Salt and pepper or seasonings you prefer
1/4 cup catsup
1/2 cup water

Mix all ingredients together except catsup and water. Make into meatballs and place in baking dish. Mix catsup and water and pour over the meatballs. Bake 45 minutes at 350 degrees. These are great served with scalloped potatoes.

Lemon juice or vinegar added in small amounts to the water will whiten boiled potatoes.

COUNTRY LAMB CASSEROLE

6 lamb chops
1/2 pound bacon, chopped
1 large onion, sliced
1 cup celery, chopped
1/2 cup green pepper, chopped
1 1/2 tablespoons flour
2 cups chicken bouillon
1 tablespoon Worcestershire sauce
1/4 cup catsup

Fry bacon pieces in large, heavy pan. Remove bacon and brown lamb chops. Remove lamb chops and saute vegetables. Add flour, then bouillon, stirring until starting to boil. Stir in Worcestershire and catsup. Place meats in casserole dish. Pour vegetable mixture over all. Cover and bake in 350 degree oven for 2 hours or until chops are very tender.

Sprinkle a little salt in the frying pan before cooking. It keeps the spatters to a minimum.

CHICKEN'N RICE PAN

1 large frying chicken
2 cups water
1 1/2 cups rice
1 package dry onion soup mix
1 can cream of chicken soup
1 can mushroom soup
1 cup milk

Place water, onion soup mix and rice in a 9x13 baking dish. Lay chicken on top. Heat chicken and mushroom soups with milk. Pour over chicken. Bake 2 hours at 350 degrees, 1 hour covered with foil, 1 hour uncovered.

And Noah he often said to his wife when he sat down to dine, I don't care where the water goes if it doesn't get into the wine. Chesterfield

"BATTER UP" FISH

Fish Fillets
Club soda
Pancake flour
Salt and pepper

Mix together club soda and pancake flour until the consistency of buttermilk. Season with salt and pepper. Dip fish in regular flour then in the batter before frying.

We like to deep fat fry either walleye or catfish that has been dipped in batter. It works best to use a heavy cast iron pot on a camp stove outside as it does get hotter than your indoor deep fat fryer. But that isn't always handy, so use the cooking method of your choice. Be sure fat is hot before adding fish, and don't overload the pot. Cook until golden brown and fish is flaky inside. There always seems to be someone at the table just waiting to try the first batch for "doneness".

Lemon juice helps take the fishy smell from hands or pans. Lemons produce more juice if soaked in hot water. If you need only a few drops of juice, prick one end with a fork and squeeze out the amount you need.

OVEN BUFFALO STROGANOFF

Mollie gave me this recipe. She made *beef* stroganoff, but it works great using the meat of your choice. It makes a really moist buffalo dish.

3 pounds buffalo stew meat
1 package onion soup mix
2 cans mushroom soup
3/4 cup chicken bouillon

Mix together and cook in a covered casserole or oven safe dish at 325 degrees for 2 1/2 hour. Then cook 1 hour more at 350 degrees, removing lid during last 20 minutes of cooking.

He that would thrive must rise at five.
He that hath thriven may lie 'till seven.
Clarke

BARBECUED HAMBURGERS FOR 20

3 tablespoons shortening
3 pounds ground beef
3 large onions, finely chopped
1 clove garlic, minced
1 tablespoon salt
1 1/2 teaspoons black pepper
2 teaspoons chili powder
2 teaspoons Worcestershire sauce
1/4 cup flour
1 1/4 cups canned tomatoes
3/4 cup catsup

Brown onions and garlic in shortening. Add beef and brown. Add seasonings. Stir in flour. Add tomatoes and catsup. Simmer 15 to 20 minutes. Serve on buns.

Old time formula for stiffening lace or crocheted doily: Make a syrup of 1 cup sugar and 1/2 cup water. Boil for 2 minutes. Dip item and shape.

MIGHTY EASY MEAT LOAF

1 1/2 pounds ground beef
1 egg
1 cup seasoned bread dressing mix
1 can onion soup
1/2 teaspoon salt

Bake 30 minutes at 350 degrees. This is a favorite of Jerry's Mother, and Jerry's Father, too, I'm sure!

Remedy: best way to relieve a chest cold was to apply onion poultices. Seems it would have been an asset to also have a nasal cold!

Homesteaders would apply poultices to snake bite wounds either on themselves or on their animals. Some were simple formulas such as applying soda and vinegar. The mixture was to be kept bubbling out of the wound for at least an hour. Or they would apply a paste of 1 tablespoon salt, 1 tablespoon soda and the yolk of an egg.

This one was rather complicated: Shoot a bird or chicken, split open and apply, while warm, to the bite. Change birds as often as necessary! It was also suggested that brandy could be used to numb the pain and to give courage. Makes one wonder who needed the brandy most!

RATTLESNAKE STEAKS

Rattlesnake steaks
Egg, beaten
Seasoned flour

Dip steaks in flour, then in egg, and again in flour. Fry in butter or oil until golden and tender. Hope you like them! **I** would serve a lot of **other** main dishes, too!

My father was the rural mail carrier from Reliance to the Lower Brule Reservation. He tells of seeing a cloud of dust and a team and wagon rushing toward the main road that he traveled to deliver mail. Dad waited as it looked like they were trying to stop him. A young boy had been bitten by a rattler, and they were trying to stop my Father to get their son to town for medical help. Many things besides mail were delivered by that mailman!

What's one man's poison, is another's meat and drink.
Beaumont and Fletcher

TUNA RICE PATTIES

We all need a quick and easy recipe when there's nothing but a can of tuna in the cupboard.

1 can well drained tuna
1 egg, beaten
1/2 cup cooked rice
1/4 cup Parmesan cheese
1/4 cup pancake mix
1/4 cup chopped green pepper
Salt and pepper to taste
Oil for frying

Mix all ingredients except oil. Make into patties. Fry six to seven minutes on each side at medium heat. Makes seven to eight patties.

The trouble with people is not that they don't know but that they know so much that ain't so. *Josh Billings*

PHEASANT SAUSAGE

Pheasant breast
Side pork or bacon
Seasoned flour

Grind equal amounts of pheasant breast with side pork or bacon. This can then be made into patties. Roll them in flour that has salt and pepper added. Brown in a hot skillet on both sides. Turn down the heat and add 1/4 cup of water for each 8 patties. Let them cook slowly for at least 20 minutes. Edna says these are tasty with pancakes and homemade syrup.

The Gunderson family owns and operates the ***G&C Pheasant Farm*** at Chamberlain, South Dakota. They work exceptionally hard raising the pheasants, actually starting with the eggs! The most enjoyable part of the year is fall when they provide hunters with excellent hunting plus a family atmosphere and great down-home cooking. Edna Gunderson shared her pheasant sausage recipe with us. It is a favorite recipe of their many repeat hunters.

HAM AND NOODLE CASSEROLE

This is a tasty casserole when you want to use up that leftover ham.

8 ounce package noodles
4 tablespoons butter
1 medium onion, chopped
1/4 teaspoon steak sauce
Salt and pepper to taste
4 ounce can mushrooms
1 tablespoon flour
2 1/2 cups tomatoes
2 cups diced ham
1/2 cup celery, diced
3/4 cup cheese
1/2 cup chopped fresh bread

Cook and drain noodles. In a slow skillet (300 degrees) toast bread in 2 tablespoons of the butter. Remove. Add the other two tablespoons butter. Saute onion, mushrooms and celery until tender. Blend in flour, salt and pepper. Add tomatoes, noodles and ham. Simmer 20 minutes. Add cheese and bread and heat through.

*PRAIRIE OYSTERS**

Calf fries
Seasoned flour
Oil

If you are a connoisseur of this delicacy, you may already have a favorite cooking method. Oysters should be skinned. If they are large I would recommend cutting them into steaks about 1/2 inch thick. These can then be floured or breaded and chicken fried in a heavy skillet.

*Calf Fries

Our immediate family thought the eating of prairie oysters was one of the very "gross" things in life and shuddered at the thought of even touching them! We found it a challenge dodging them as they sailed through the air when Dad was "tending" calves each year. But a neighbor boy thought that was a waste of good "oysters" and rigged up the best way to cook them. He started a wood fire in an old barrel and then strung the oysters on a stick that would set across the top of the barrel. They were "done just right" when the skins began to pop!

"DILL"ICIOUS BURGER DISH

1 1/2 pounds hamburger
6 onion slices, 1/4 inch thick
Salt and pepper
18 dill pickle slices
1 can tomato soup
2 tablespoons Worcestershire sauce

Make up 12 patties. Sprinkle with salt and pepper. Place one onion slice and three pickle slices on six patties. Place remaining six patties on top and press edges together to seal. Put in flat baking dish, but do not layer. Combine soup with sauce and pour over meat. Bake 45 minutes at 375 degrees.

Do not do unto others as you would they should do unto you. Their tastes may not be the same. Shaw

HOT DOG AND POTATO SKILLET

Late getting home and the kids are crabby? Here's a quick recipe they will really enjoy.

1/4 cup margarine
4 large potatoes, sliced
1 medium onion, sliced
1/2 cup chopped green pepper
1/4 cup pimiento
1 cup chopped dill pickles
1/4 cup pickle juice
1/2 pound hot dogs, sliced
Salt and pepper to taste

Fry potatoes and onion until browned. Add rest of ingredients and simmer for 15 minutes, stirring occasionally.

Have you ever had two glasses stick together? Fill the inside glass with cold water and place the outside glass in hot water to separate them.

MEDICINE CREEK EGG SCRAMBLE

1 cup diced bacon
1/4 cup chopped onion
3 ounces mushrooms
1/8 teaspoon paprika
12 beaten eggs
2 1/4 cups bread crumbs (3-4 slices)
2 tablespoons butter
2 tablespoons flour
1/2 teaspoon salt
1/8 teaspoon pepper
2 cups milk
1 cup colby cheese, shredded

Cook bacon until almost done. Add onions and cook until tender. Add eggs and scramble until set. In separate saucepan prepare cheese sauce by melting butter and blending in flour, salt and pepper. Add milk and stir until bubbly. Stir in cheese. Fold mushrooms and cooked egg mixture into the cheese sauce. Put in 9 x 13 greased pan. Combine crumbs with additional melted butter to consistency you like and sprinkle on top. Sprinkle with paprika. Cover and chill until ready to bake, up to 2 days ahead. Bake at 350 degrees for 45 minutes.

VENISON AND SAUSAGE MEATBALLS

1 1/2 pounds meat
(3/4 pound ground venison,
3/4 pound pork sausage)
1 cup chopped onion
1/4 cup flour
1 teaspoon salt
1/8 teaspoon black pepper
2 1/2 cups milk
1 box frozen peas
1 large can mushrooms, drained

Mix venison and sausage together. Make into small meatballs. Brown in heavy skillet, adding shortening only if necessary. Remove meatballs. Brown the onion. While these brown, cook the frozen peas. Add flour, salt and pepper to onion and drippings mixture. Blend well. Stir in milk and cook until it thickens. Add the drained peas and mushrooms plus the meatballs. Simmer at least 20 minutes.

Do you *want your egg whites to whip up really nice - let them come to room temperature before beating.*

PINEAPPLED PORK

6 slices bacon
6 pork chops
Salt and pepper
1/2 cup water
1 tablespoon sugar
1 teaspoon cornstarch
6 pineapple slices, drained
1/2 cup pineapple syrup
1 tablespoon vinegar
1/4 cup raisins

Brown bacon slices in large skillet and remove. Brown pork chops, seasoning with salt and pepper as desired. Add water. Cover and simmer until chops are tender. Remove chops. Mix the sugar and cornstarch into the syrup. Add with vinegar and raisins to drippings in pan. Heat until thickened. Lay chops back in pan, placing a bacon slice and ring of pineapple on each. Spoon the sauce over the chops. Cover and cook until heated through.

CORN CHOWDER

4 large potatoes, diced
1 onion, chopped
1/2 cup chopped green pepper
2 carrots, sliced
2 cups celery, sliced
3 cups water
1 cup ham, diced
1 can cream-style corn
1 can whole kernel corn
1 quart milk
1 can evaporated milk
2 teaspoons salt
1/2 teaspoon pepper
Flour

Place first six ingredients in large soup pot and simmer until tender. Add remaining ingredients except flour and bring just to a simmer. You can adjust the liquids to make a thick or thin chowder. I like a very thick chowder so usually make a paste with several tablespoons of flour and a little water. Stir this in as it heats.

SOUR CREAM BEEF STEW

2 pounds beef stew meat
1 large onion, chopped
1 garlic clove, minced
Oil
4 cups water
4 large carrots, sliced thick
6 medium potatoes, chopped
1 teaspoon salt
1/2 teaspoon black pepper
1 carton sour cream
Flour to thicken
or 2 tablespoons roux*

Brown stew meat, onions and garlic in oil. Add the water, carrots, potatoes, salt and pepper. Simmer until meat is tender. Stir in the sour cream and thicken with as much flour as is needed to make a nice, thick stew. Simmer a few more minutes before serving. This is great with baking powder biscuits and a green salad.

*Recipe on page 51

PRAIRIE PASTA

This is a wonderful pasta recipe sent to me by my friend, Fr. John.

1 pound pasta
1 1/2 pounds bacon, cooked crisp
2 onions, chopped
3 to 4 cloves garlic
1 1/2 pounds mushrooms
1 pint half and half cream
1/2 cup Parmesan cheese
2 eggs, beaten

Crumble fried bacon and set aside. Saute onions, mushrooms and garlic in bacon grease. Remove and set aside. Cook pasta. Combine cream, cheese and eggs and add to hot pasta. Toss until well coated.

Place grains of rice in salt shakers to keep salt from absorbing dampness.

SALMON CASSEROLE

1 1/2 cups cooked rice
1 package frozen peas
1 can salmon, including liquid
2 eggs, beaten
1/2 cup milk
Salt and pepper
1 cup grated cheese
1 cup crushed potato chips

Place half of rice in bottom of casserole dish. Add frozen peas, then flaked salmon with liquid. Place remainder of rice over salmon. Season with salt and pepper. Mix eggs and milk together and pour over top. Bake approximately 1/2 hour at 375 degrees. Add cheese and potato chips on top and return to oven to melt. Let stand for a while before serving so that it sets.

BLT SOUP

1 pound bacon, cooked and crumbled
1/2 cup onion, chopped
Tomatoes, your choice, to make 2 quarts
4 beef bouillon cubes
1/4 teaspoon baking soda
1 quart medium white sauce
Shredded lettuce
Sun dried tomatoes

Saute onion in bacon grease. Add onion and bouillon with bacon to the tomatoes and bring just to a simmer. Stir in soda. Stir tomato mixture into the hot white sauce. Top each bowl with shredded lettuce and sun dried tomatoes.

ROUX

Roux is a good basis for all your stews or gumbos.

1 cup oil or 1 cup margarine
1 cup flour (or substitute pancake flour)

Heat oil, gradually adding flour. Stir until well mixed. Lower heat and stir until medium brown. Dissolve in warm water to use.

A DOZEN SLOPPY JOES

2 pounds ground beef
1 large onion, chopped
2 cups celery, chopped
1 green pepper, chopped fine
1 cup catsup
2 cups water
1 can tomato soup
1/4 cup vinegar
1 teaspoon dry mustard
2 tablespoons brown sugar
1 tablespoon Worcestershire sauce
1 teaspoon salt
1 teaspoon chili powder
1/2 teaspoon garlic powder
1/2 teaspoon pepper

Brown ground beef. Add all other ingredients and simmer for at least 1/2 hour before serving.

COLD TATER BAKE

Have you heard about having to "take an old cold tater and wait"? Wouldn't be so bad if you could have one this way!

Leftover potatoes
1 cup cucumber dressing
1 cup shredded cheddar cheese
1 cup cubed cooked ham
Paprika
Dill pickles

Slice leftover potatoes to fill a casserole dish. Mix in other ingredients, sprinkle with paprika and bake until heated through in medium oven. Serve with lots of dill pickles!

Use paste wax to remove tar from floors, shoes, etc.

CLAM CHOWDER

1/4 pound bacon, diced
1 cup chopped onion
5 cups water
1 cup chopped celery
1 cup chopped carrots
2 cups diced potatoes
2 cans minced clams
2 13-ounce cans evaporated milk
1 teaspoon salt
1/4 teaspoon pepper

Brown bacon in a dutch oven. Remove and cook onion. Add the water, celery, carrots and potatoes, simmering for 1 hour. Add clams and bacon pieces. Simmer for a short time, then add milk, salt and pepper. Heat and serve with oyster crackers.

A Taste of Prairie Life

...GETABLE SOUP

...ans
...stewed tomatoes
...omatoes
...ic powder
...nd oregano
...lt and pepper, if desired

Put into a big pot. Boil at medium temperature. Then cook for one hour.

Shandra was 10 years old when she gave me this recipe. She makes this with her dad, Tim. He says they use any vegetables they have on hand.

TACO SO

2 pounds hamburger
1 cup onion, chopped
1 large can chili beans
1 can corn
1 large can tomatoes
1 large can tomato sauce
1 package taco seasoning

Brown hamburger and onion. Add remaining ingredients and simmer. Serve with grated cheese, sour cream and crushed taco chips.

Use equal parts of flour and cornstarch to make gravy.

TRAVIS'S MEXICAN OMELETTE

Chorizo sausage or a spicy sausage
1/4 cup green onions, sliced
1 cup sliced fresh mushrooms
1 tomato, chopped
1 cup cheddar cheese, shredded
4 eggs, beaten
1/4 cup milk
Salt and pepper to taste

Saute sausage, onions, mushrooms and tomato. Add eggs and scramble. Fold in the cheese. Serve topped with sour cream and salsa.

ROAST BEEF AND DRESSING

3-4 pound roast
2 eggs
2 cups dry bread crumbs
2 cups corn flakes
2 cups uncooked hamburger
1 large onion, diced
1 teaspoon sage
1/2 teaspoon salt
1/4 teaspoon pepper
1 can cream of mushroom soup

Place roast in a large baking pan. Combine the rest of the ingredients except the soup. Place the dressing over roast. Cover with soup. Cover pan and bake until roast is almost done. Remove the lid and bake another 1/2 hour.

TRACY'S SPAGHETTI SAUCE

1 pound pork sausage
1 onion, chopped
1 teaspoon minced garlic
4 small zucchini, sliced
1 quart jar canned tomatoes
1 jar chunky pepper and mushroom spaghetti sauce

Brown the sausage and drain. Add the rest of the ingredients, bring to a boil and simmer for 30 minutes.

Note: Jerry thinks this is the best sauce he has ever eaten.

WILD RICE SOUP

2/3 cup wild rice, rinsed
3 strips bacon, fried and crumbled
1 small onion, diced
1/2 cup carrots, grated
1/2 cup celery, diced
4 cups chicken broth
1 to 1 1/2 cups half and half cream
1 tablespoon butter
1 tablespoon flour
Salt and pepper to taste
Dill weed

Fry bacon. Save enough grease to saute rice, onion, carrots and celery for five minutes. Remove and place these plus bacon in soup kettle. Stir in broth and heat until boiling. Reduce heat and simmer until rice is tender, about one hour. Stir in half and half. Mix butter and flour and whisk into the soup. Stir until soup thickens. Season, adding dill weed if desired.

OLD FASHIONED STRUDELS

1 pound kielbasa, sliced, or
2-3 cooked pork chops, chopped
1 can sauerkraut
1 loaf frozen bread dough, or
use your favorite bread dough

Fry kielbasa or pork chop pieces in large fry pan. Add drained sauerkraut and cook until it all browns. Pat out the thawed dough as if you were making cinnamon rolls. Spread sauerkraut and kielbasa on the dough, roll up and seal. Slice as for rolls, 2 1/2 to 3 inches thick. Place a cup of liquid, water or water and sauerkraut juice mix, plus a tablespoon of shortening in skillet. Set strudels in loosely, partially cover and let cook down, approximately 10 minutes. When browned nicely on the bottom, turn and finish cooking. This will take another 15 minutes. Add a little water if necessary. Be sure to watch these carefully as Marcia tells me she burns them every time!

GRILLED WALLEYE

Fish fillets
Salt
Pepper
Cooking oil
Bacon slices

Fillet fish lengthwise. Wipe both sides of fillet with cooking oil and salt and pepper well. Wrap a slice of bacon several times around each piece. Place in a grill basket and grill until bacon is cooked. When bacon is cooked, the fish is done. Allow 20 to 30 minutes.

GRILLED CORN

6 ears corn, husks and silks removed
1/4 cup butter or margarine, melted
1/4 teaspoon salt
1 teaspoon Italian seasoning
1/8 teaspoon pepper

Roll fresh corn in the remaining ingredients and wrap tightly in heavy aluminum foil. Grill corn over medium fire for about 30 minutes, turning several times.

DONNA'S DEVILED BEEF STEW

1 1/2 pounds cubed beef
Shortening
2 tablespoons flour
1 teaspoon salt
1 teaspoon paprika
3 tablespoons butter
1 cup minced onion
1 bouillon cube
1 1/2 cups boiling water
1 teaspoon powdered mustard
2 teaspoons horseradish
1/2 cup sour cream

Melt shortening in large fry pan. Add the beef that has been rolled in the flour. Add salt and paprika. Melt butter in a small skillet and saute the onion. Dissolve bouillon in water and add with the onion to the stew meat. Add mustard and horseradish. Cook slowly until done, which will take at least an hour. Add sour cream just before serving. Serve on rice or noodles.

MICROWAVE MEAT LOAF

2 pounds ground beef
1 egg
1/4 cup quick oatmeal
1/4 cup milk
2 tablespoons chopped onions
2 tablespoons brown sugar
1/4 teaspoon nutmeg
1/8 teaspoon allspice
1/2 teaspoon salt
1/8 teaspoon pepper
2/3 cup catsup
2 tablespoons brown sugar
1 1/2 teaspoons dry mustard

Combine all ingredients except catsup, brown sugar and dry mustard. Put in covered microwave pan with a small glass in the center. Microwave for 8-10 minutes on full power, turning dish once during cooking. Drain off fat. Top with this sauce made of last three ingredients. Return to microwave for 6 minutes on full power. This recipe from Alice Olson of the Old West Museum is so good and easy!

Life on the prairie by early settlers of SD was not one of comfort; just step into the original claim shanty used by the grandparents of Gene Olson on the grounds of ***Old West Museum***, Chamberlain, SD. This one room shanty was home to a growing family in the area of Pukwana, South Dakota.

Some reminiscings of my Father about his family:

"Early day experiences of a pioneer family: They moved to this unimproved place 10 miles northwest of Lower Brule in the Little Bend area and built a one room "tar paper" shack. It had no floor except for horse hides. A chicken coop was made at the top end of a washout. The door to this was at the lower end, and steps were cut in the embankment to get to the coop door. Their young son was having a sporting good time chasing the chickens one morning and tumbled down these steps, breaking his leg. The oldest daughter rode 3 miles to the closest neighbors, and they rode seven more miles to the Lower Brule Indian Agency where there was a young government doctor. He made the 10 mile trip in a one horse carriage and set the leg and splinted it up. He must have been a good doctor as the leg healed perfectly.

Some years later: A daughter, her husband and a sister were attempting to get started in ranching. They lived 2 miles from the river and, as they had to water the livestock, it was necessary to take them every other day to drink. Holes had to be chopped through the ice to drink from. Then one day a cow didn't want to wait for the holes to be chopped so went on out farther to an open "air hole" and was followed by others. They skidded on the ice into the air hole. The water was deep and swift, and they desperately tried to climb out but, of course, couldn't make it. They vanished under the ice at the end of the air hole."

STEAK BISTECHINE

4 8-ounce sirloin steaks
2 tablespoons olive oil
1 tablespoon butter
1 teaspoon garlic, chopped
1/4 teaspoon black pepper
1/2 teaspoon chopped basil

SEASONED CROUTON:
4 sections French bread
4 tablespoons butter
4 anchovies
1/8 teaspoon white pepper

SAUCE:
2 cups burgundy wine
3 cups thin brown gravy
1 cup sliced mushrooms

GARNISH:
Chopped green onions

Saute steaks to required doneness in the olive oil with the butter, garlic and pepper. Remove steak and hold in oven at 200 degrees. Make up the sauce. Deglaze the skillet with the red wine. Add sliced mushrooms and reduce to half. Whip the butter for the croutons with the white pepper and anchovies. Spread on the French bread and broil to golden brown. Place sirloins on these croutons. Ladle sauce over sirloins and top with the green onions.

Cheryl Jordan comes from "Big Sky Country, Montana." She has been enjoying the "tastes" of her trade for 25 years. From her family restaurant, the gourmet room "Quentinellis," to banquet manager at Cedar Shore Resort at Chamberlain, SD, she has shared her cooking ideas, her cheese carved pheasants and special painted plate desserts featuring chocolate geese, bugling elk and pheasants. Thanks, Cheryl, for sharing this special recipe.

WALLEYE FISH FRITTERS

Walleye fillets cut in bite size pieces
Green pepper, chopped
Onions, chopped
Beer
Flour
Salt
Pepper

Make up a beer batter using beer and flour, seasoned with salt and pepper. The batter should be thick, like the consistency of dumplings. Mix in the fish, green pepper and onions. Drop from a spoon into 375 degree oil and cook until golden brown.

Ron Schara acquired this recipe from a fishing guide that took him to the Lake of the Woods. Ron is a newspaper columnist for the Minneapolis Star Tribune and TV host for the show, "Minnesota Bound."

MORE MEAT AND TATERS:

Bread Basket Upset

Fry Bread
Indian Tacos
Wozapi
Sponge Bread
Sour Dough Starter
Sour Dough Pancakes
Hush Puppies
Homemade Pancakes
Homemade Syrup
Oven French Toast
Mincemeat Bread
Granola Bread
Oatmeal Apple Raisin Muffins
Soda Biscuits
Poppy Seed Bread
Krispies
Bread Bowls
Better Banana Bread
Grandma Mabel's Raised Donuts
Ground Beef Bread
Ranch House Muffins
Light As A Prairie Breeze Biscuits
Pretzels
Garden Corn Bread
Flower Pot Breads and Muffins
Batter Rolls

FRY BREAD

2 cups self-rising flour
1/2 cup nonfat dry milk powder
1 cup warm water

Combine above ingredients. Knead for a short while. Shape into balls that you can flatten into rounds. Fry until golden brown on first side, turn and brown for a short amount of time on second side.

INDIAN TACOS

Keep the fry bread rounds warm after frying. Top with your favorite ingredients. Here are some suggestions:

Cooked ground beef, drained and seasoned
Shredded cheese
Chopped lettuce
Minced onion
Ripe olives
Chopped tomatoes
Green chilies
Taco sauce, salsa or picante sauce
Sour cream
Refried or kidney beans

WOZAPI

This is a delicious "sauce" in which you can dip your fry bread.

1 package frozen strawberries in syrup
1/4-1/2 cup flour

Thaw strawberries. You may need to use up to the 1/2 cup flour if the package of strawberries has a lot of juice. Mix the flour into a small amount of the juice until it is not lumpy. Stir this into the strawberries. Cook and stir until it thickens.

This was traditionally made with berries, sweetened and thickened to a pudding-like consistency. It would have pieces of tallow added for flavoring.

SPONGE BREAD

1 package yeast
1/4 cup warm water
1/4 cup flour
1 small cooked potato, mashed in
1 cup hot potato water
1 tablespoon sugar

Dissolve yeast in water. Add the rest of the ingredients and let set overnight.

1 cup flour
1 cup scalded milk, cooled
2 teaspoons salt
1 tablespoon sugar
2 tablespoons shortening, melted

Beat the above ingredients into the yeast sponge. Then add:

1 1/4 quarts flour, approximately

Knead. Let rise to double (twice if you have time). Place in two greased loaf pans. When it has raised, bake 10 minutes at 425 degrees and 45 minutes at 375 degrees.

Ed Werner was a short stocky man who spent much of his life on the Lower Brule Reservation in central South Dakota. His hearty nature was evident from his youth as he stowed away on a ship to America while in his teens.

He loved pancakes, and his pancakes were infamous - maybe not for their quality as much as for his method of making them. It must have been a *form* of *sour dough* in that crusty bowl sitting on the stove. He just added eggs and flour in the center and stirred - mostly eggs! And he continued to use it until the hole in the center was too small to make up any more batter.

I must have gotten my love of pancakes from my Grandpa!

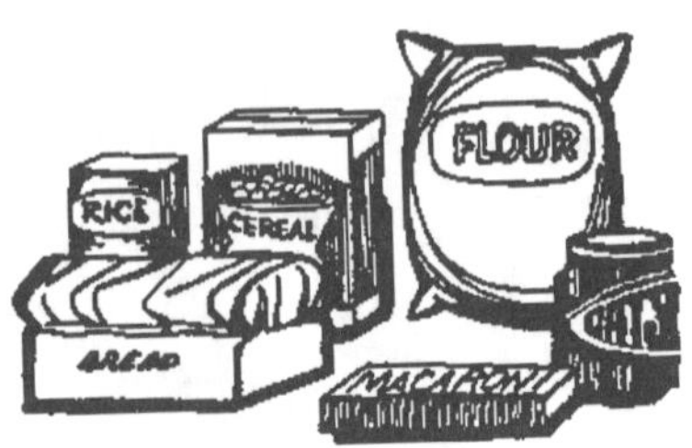

BEER SOUR DOUGH STARTER

2 cups flour
2 tablespoons sugar
1 package yeast
1 cup water, warm
1 can beer

Mix together flour and sugar and add to yeast dissolved in the water. Add the beer and beat well until lumps disappear. Place in crock and let stand in warm place until mixture has soured and is foamy. Cover and refrigerate until needed. Add a cup of water, cup of flour and 1 tablespoon sugar to mixture when you use some out of the starter. Stir it in and let set out until frothy before returning to refrigerator.

There are many sour dough starter recipes some as basic as using just flour and water while others have added ingredients to enhance the "souring process". Hope you like this one!

SOUR DOUGH PANCAKES

1 cup sour dough starter
1 cup flour
1 teaspoon sugar
1/2 teaspoon baking soda
1/2 teaspoon salt
1 egg, well beaten
1/2 cup water
2 tablespoons shortening, melted

Take the sour dough starter out of the refrigerator and let it set out for a while before mixing with other ingredients. Mix dry ingredients together. Add the starter, egg and water. Stir in the shortening. Fry as you would any pancake mixture. Serve while warm with butter and syrup. Or you might like to try these with chokecherry syrup - see Good Old Days section.

HUSH PUPPIES

1 cup cornmeal
1 cup self-rising flour
1 tablespoon dried onion flakes
1 egg
1 cup buttermilk
1/2 teaspoon sugar
1/4 teaspoon salt

Mix ingredients until blended well. Cook these by dropping spoons of batter into deep fat and cooking until nicely browned. Great served with fish!

Frozen bread dough will thaw in five minutes in a paper sack in a 325 degree oven.

HOMEMADE PANCAKES

On a Saturday morning try out this homemade pancake recipe from Ruth. Serve it up with her syrup and some crispy bacon - but make plenty as the aroma will bring all the neighbors over for brunch!

2 cups flour
1 egg
4 teaspoons baking powder
2 tablespoons white sugar
1 teaspoon salt
1/3 cup cooking oil
1 1/2 cups milk

Mix together until smooth. Fry on high (425 degrees), preferably in electric fry pan in which you have placed a small amount of cooking oil.

HOMEMADE SYRUP

1 cup white sugar
1/2 cup brown sugar
3/4 cup water
1/4 cup corn syrup

Mix together and boil 2 minutes. Keeps well in refrigerator.

OVEN FRENCH TOAST

3 eggs
3/4 cup milk
1 tablespoon sugar
1/4 teaspoon salt
Vanilla to taste
8 slices English muffin toasting bread

Heat oven to 500 degrees. Butter a cookie sheet or use a non-stick pan. Beat eggs, milk, sugar and salt with fork. Heat cookie sheet in oven for one minute. Remove from oven. Dip bread into egg mixture and arrange on hot cookie sheet. Drizzle remaining egg mixture over bread. Bake until bottoms are golden brown, 5 to 8 minutes. Turn bread. Bake 2 to 4 minutes longer until golden brown.

This is a recipe from Linda and Merrill of the ***Diamond Dot Ranch.*** Of course pheasant is their favorite cuisine! If you want great upland bird hunting, including the wily ringneck pheasant, prairie chicken, dove, partridge and sharp tail grouse, coupled with prairie and river break scenery and South Dakota hospitality, contact them at the Diamond Dot Ranch, HCR 5, Box 11, Reliance, SD 57569.

MINCEMEAT BREAD

Rind of one orange, grated
Juice of one orange
Boiling water
2 tablespoons butter
1 cup sugar
1 egg
2 cups flour
1/4 teaspoon salt
1 teaspoon baking powder
1 teaspoon soda
1 cup mincemeat
1/2 cup chopped nuts

Place orange juice and rind in cup and fill to brim with boiling water. Cream butter. Add sugar. Mix and add egg. Add orange mixture and dry ingredients, mixing well. Add mincemeat and nuts. Bake in a two pound bread pan that has been well greased. Bake 50 to 60 minutes at 350 degrees.

If your house looks like a true roach heaven, try poisoning them with a mixture of 1 part boric acid powder, 1/2 part sugar mixed into 2 parts flour.

GRANOLA BREAD

2 packages yeast
2 cups warm water
2 cups granola, crushed
1/2 cup brown sugar
1 tablespoon salt
2 eggs
1/4 cup oil
5 cups flour

Dissolve yeast in water. Stir in all other items, reserving 2 cups flour. Mix in more flour, enough to make a stiff dough that is easy to handle. Knead 8 to 10 minutes. Place in greased bowl and let rise until doubled, about one hour. Make into three loaves. Place in loaf pans and bake 30 to 35 minutes at 375 degrees. Brush tops with butter.

Old time remedy for arthritis: 1/2 hour before meals, drink a glass of milk in which you put a teaspoon of cod liver oil.

OATMEAL APPLE RAISIN MUFFINS

Mary Liz's healthy muffins for hungry people.

2 egg whites
1/2 cup applesauce
3/4 cup skim milk
1 cup raisins
1 apple, chopped
1 cup quick oats
3 teaspoons baking powder
1 teaspoon nutmeg
1 cup flour
1/3 cup sugar
1 teaspoon salt
2 teaspoons cinnamon

Beat egg whites. Stir in remaining ingredients, mixing just to moisten. Pour into 12 lined or greased muffin cups until 3/4 full. Bake at 400 degrees for 15 to 20 minutes.

Keep marshmallows in the freezer. Cut them while frozen and they won't stick to your scissors or knife.

SODA BISCUITS

My Mother remembers that Grandma made soda rather than baking powder biscuits.

1 teaspoon soda
1 teaspoon salt
1 quart flour
1 cup sour cream

Combine dry ingredients. Stir in the sour cream. Roll out the dough and cut. Bake in a hot oven until tops start to brown.

POPPY SEED BREAD

3 eggs
2 1/2 cups sugar
3 cups flour
1 1/3 cups oil
1 1/2 cups milk
1 1/2 tablespoons poppy seed
1 1/2 teaspoons almond extract
1 1/2 teaspoons vanilla
1 1/2 teaspoons baking powder
1 1/2 teaspoons salt

Cream eggs and sugar and add remaining ingredients. Mix well. Divide and pour into three small greased and floured pans (8x3x2). Bake at 350 degrees for one hour. Spread with topping.

TOPPING

3/4 cup sugar
1/2 teaspoon vanilla
1/2 teaspoon almond extract
1/4 cup orange juice
2 tablespoons melted butter

Mix and pour over bread. Leave bread in pan 10 minutes before turning out.

KRISPIES

Frozen cinnamon rolls*
Sugar

Allow frozen rolls to thaw or use your own rolls, after cutting. Place on wax paper sprinkled sugar. Roll out with rolling pin, turning over into more sugar as needed until each is thin and round. Bake immediately in hot oven.

*or use your favorite cinnamon roll recipe

I was so happy to get this recipe. Krispies have always been a favorite of my Dad.

BREAD BOWLS

Shape dough over bowls, custard cups, etc. Be sure to spray the item well before covering with dough. Let rise. Bake in 375 degree oven until golden brown - time will differ depending on size of bowl you are making but this will usually take a half an hour. Use for salads, soups, chili or stews.

Make your bread bowls from frozen dough that has been allowed to thaw, a regular bread dough recipe or try this:

1 hot roll mix
1 cup mashed potatoes flakes
1 egg, beaten
1 tablespoon dried minced onions
2 tablespoons margarine, melted in
1 1/3 cups hot water

Combine ingredients, knead and let set for 10 minutes before shaping over baking items.

BETTER BANANA BREAD

4 ripe bananas
3 eggs
3/4 cup margarine
1 cup sugar
1 teaspoon vanilla
1 cup all-bran or oatmeal
1/2 cup raisins
2 1/4 cups flour
2 teaspoons soda
1/4 teaspoon salt

Combine first five items. Add remaining ingredients. Put into 2 greased and floured bread pans. Bake at 350 degrees for 20 minutes, then 25 to 30 minutes more at 300 degrees.

GRANDMA MABEL'S RAISED DONUTS

1 cup mashed potatoes
1/4 cup warm water
2 packages yeast
2 cups warmed milk
1/2 cup margarine
1 teaspoon salt
3/4 cup sugar
2 eggs, beaten
2 cups flour
5-6 cups flour

Dissolve yeast in water; then add to mashed potatoes. Mix together milk, margarine, salt, sugar and eggs and stir into yeast mixture with 2 cups of flour. Then add remaining flour until right consistency to knead. Knead well. Cover and let rise for 2 hours. Knead down and let rise again. Roll out to 1/2 inch; then cut with donut cutter and place on cookie sheets. Let rise; then fry on both sides in 375 degree oil. Drain on brown paper. Glaze if desired or dip in sugar.

GROUND BEEF BREAD

1/2 pound lean ground beef
2 cups flour
1/2 cup sugar
3 teaspoons baking powder
1 teaspoon soda
1/2 teaspoon salt
1 egg
1 cup buttermilk
3 tablespoons margarine
1 teaspoon vanilla
1/2 cup chopped nuts

Combine raw ground beef, egg, milk, margarine and vanilla. Add combined dry ingredients and nuts. Mix until moistened. Bake in greased and floured loaf pan at 350 degrees for approximately 45 minutes.

RANCH HOUSE MUFFINS

2 cups biscuit mix
1 pound cooked ground beef
1 teaspoon salt
1/2 teaspoon soda
1 beaten egg
2/3 cup orange juice
1 teaspoon grated orange peel

Add salt and soda to biscuit mix. Combine egg, orange juice and orange peel. Add to biscuit mix and stir just till moistened. Fold in meat. Bake in muffin tin at 400 degrees for 25 to 30 minutes. Makes 12 muffins.

LIGHT AS A PRAIRIE BREEZE BISCUITS

2 1/2 cups flour
1 teaspoon baking powder
or soda/baking powder mix
1 teaspoon salt
1/8 cup sugar
1/2 cup shortening
1 package dry yeast
1 cup buttermilk
1/4 cup warm water

Dissolve yeast in water. Mix dry ingredients together and cut in the shortening. Stir in buttermilk and yeast water until blended. Put in large covered bowl and refrigerate up to 3 days. When ready to use, knead. Roll into balls and place on greased pan. Bake at 400 degrees approximately 15 minutes or until done.

PRETZELS

1 envelope yeast
1 1/2 cups warm water
1 tablespoon sugar
1 teaspoon salt
4 cups flour
1 egg, beaten
Coarse salt

Dissolve yeast in water. Add the dry ingredients. Add just enough flour to make a dough you can knead. Let rise if you have time, or you can make them up right away. Make into pretzel shapes. Place on greased baking sheet. Brush with the egg and sprinkle with salt. Bake for 10-15 minutes or until golden brown.

GARDEN CORN BREAD

3/4 cup cottage cheese
3/4 cup milk
1/2 cup margarine, melted
2 eggs
1/4 cup white flour
1 1/2 cups cornmeal
1 teaspoon baking powder
1/4 teaspoon salt
1/2 cup grated zucchini
1/4 cup chopped onion
1/4 cup chopped carrots

Blend cottage cheese, milk, margarine and eggs. Add dry ingredients, then vegetables. Mix well. Grease an 8-inch baking pan liberally. Bake approximately 25 minutes at 375 degrees.

Run out of deodorant? Here's a homemade recipe that would work in an emergency. Mix together 2 tablespoons alum and one pint of water.

FLOWER POT BREADS AND MUFFINS

Tracy gave me some great flower pots made to use for baking. They have a special lining, but you can buy 3-inch clay pots and season them so they can be used for baking. You should first bake them 45 minutes in a hot oven. Remove from oven and liberally cover with vegetable oil. Put back in the oven for at least 30 minutes.

Fill the pots half full of bread dough and let rise or use your favorite muffin or spoon bread or quick bread recipe - try the recipe on the next page!

If you are boiling eggs and one floats, discard it as that would indicate it is stale.

BATTER ROLLS

2 cups lukewarm water
1 package dry yeast
3/4 cup shortening, melted
4 cups self-rising flour
4 tablespoons sugar
1 egg, beaten

Mix yeast into water. Add shortening. Place in large bowl and stir in remaining ingredients. Spoon batter into well greased muffin tins. Bake immediately at 425 degrees for 20 minutes. This batter will also keep in refrigerator for 2-3 days.

MORE BREADS:

Fixin's from the Garden

Super Slaw
Oriental Style Salad Dressing
Cheesy Salad Dressing
Beet Salad
Lime Marshmallow Delight
Fruit and Cheese Salad
Cranberry Relish Salad
Rice and Fruit Salad
Baked Potatoes
Roasted Garlic
Dina's Angel Bake
Slaw Dressing
Country Corn Bake
Favorite Mixed Vegetable Casserole
Frozen "Canned" Fruit Salad
Orange and Onion Spinach Salad
Sesame Almond Slaw
Potluck Salad
Garlic Mashed Potatoes
Great Corn Off The Cob
Fresh Corn Salad
Green Chile Bake
Waldorf Salad
Onion Patties
Cranberry Delight

SUPER SLAW

1 head cabbage, chopped fine
1 large onion, chopped fine
1/4 cup sugar

2/3 cup vinegar
2/3 cup oil
1 teaspoon salt
2 teaspoons sugar
1 teaspoon celery seed
1 tablespoon prepared mustard

Sprinkle first sugar over cabbage and onion and let stand while preparing the dressing. Cook the remaining ingredients until they come to a good boil. Pour over cabbage mixture while hot. Keeps well for several days in refrigerator.

If all the good people were clever, and all clever people were good,
the world would be nicer than ever we thought that it possibly could.
But somehow, 'tis seldom or never the two hit it off as they should;
the good are so harsh to the clever, the clever so rude to the good!
Wordsworth

ORIENTAL STYLE SALAD DRESSING

3 tablespoons salad oil
1 tablespoon vinegar
1 1/4 teaspoons soy sauce
1 1/4 teaspoons sugar
1/2 teaspoon dry mustard
1 clove garlic, crushed

Shake well.

CHEESY DRESSING

1/2 cup crumbled blue cheese
1/2 cup cottage cheese
1/2 cup mayonnaise
2 tablespoons vinegar
1/8 teaspoon salt
3 drops hot pepper sauce

Combine and chill several hours.

Vinegar added to the cooking water will help cut down on the odor when cooking items like cabbage. Maybe my smoke alarm will stop going off every time I cook pungent smelling foods!

BEET SALAD

1 can green beans
1 can diced beets
1 cup chopped onion
1/2 cup sour cream
1 tablespoon vinegar
1 teaspoon sugar
Salt and pepper

Drain beans and beets. Combine all ingredients and chill two hours.

The rain it raineth on the just and also on the unjust fella; But chiefly on the just, because the unjust steals the just's umbrella. Sichel

LIME MARSHMALLOW DELIGHT

1 small package lime gelatin
1 small package lemon gelatin
2 cups boiling water
1 cup cold water
1 cup applesauce

DRESSING

9 large marshmallows
1 cup whipping cream
1 small package cream cheese

Dissolve gelatin in boiling water. Add cold water and applesauce and let set. Make up the dressing by letting the marshmallows stand in the cream to soften. Add softened cream cheese and whip. Spread on gelatin.

To remove iron rust stains from material, boil in 8 teaspoons cream of tartar for each quart of water. Rinse.

FRUIT AND CHEESE SALAD

2 packages orange gelatin
2 cups hot water
1 cup reserved juice
3/4 cup mini marshmallows
1 large can apricots
1 medium can crushed pineapple

TOPPING

1/2 cup sugar
2 tablespoons flour
1 egg, beaten
1 cup reserved juice
2 tablespoons butter
1 cup cream, whipped
3/4 cup cheddar cheese, grated

Dissolve gelatin in water. Add juice. When partly congealed, fold in chopped apricots and pineapple, both of which have been well drained. When firm, add topping. Combine the sugar and flour and blend in egg. Gradually stir in juice. Cook over low heat until thickened. Stir in butter and cool. Fold in the whipped cream and spread over gelatin. Sprinkle with cheese.

CRANBERRY RELISH SALAD

1 quart fresh cranberries, ground
1 cup crushed pineapple
1 1/2 cups sugar
1/2 pound marshmallows, small
1 cup cream, whipped

Combine and let set several hours or overnight in refrigerator.

When June is come, then all the day I'll sit with my love in the scented hay; And watch the sunshot palaces high that the white clouds built in the breezy sky. *Bridges*

RICE AND FRUIT SALAD

1 small box cherry gelatin
2 cups water
1 1/2 cups cooked rice
1/4 cup sugar
1 teaspoon vanilla
1 cup cream, whipped
1 cup pineapple or fruit cocktail

Make up gelatin according to directions. Let set until hard, then whip. Fold in remaining ingredients and return to refrigerator until firm. Many of my recipes I have had for a long time. They call for whipping cream. Usually I have the non-dairy whipped topping on hand and use it.

If your recipe calls for self-rising flour and you don't have any in your larder, not to worry! Just add 1/2 teaspoon salt and 1/2 tablespoon baking powder to each cup of flour.

BAKED POTATOES AND ROASTED GARLIC

Both potatoes and garlic taste best to me if coated with oil or shortening and salted before oven roasting.

Scrub potatoes well and soak in salt water before baking. Oil the potatoes and sprinkle with coarse salt. I like to bake the potatoes at a high oven heat.

Elephant garlic is a delicious variety to roast. Remove outermost skin from garlic. Cover with oil or shortening and sprinkle liberally with salt. Roast garlic at a slower oven temperature, medium heat or lower; until you can feel that it is soft when it is squeezed between your fingers. Garlic is delicious served with meat or just spread on crackers or hearty bread.

DINA'S ANGEL BAKE

1 can cream style corn
1 can whole kernel corn
1/4 pound butter, melted
1/2 red pepper, diced
1/2 bag angel hair pasta, crumbled dry
1/2 cup chopped onion

Combine above ingredients in casserole dish and bake at 325 degrees for 1/2 hour or until pasta is done and the casserole has browned.

SLAW DRESSING

This is a handy dressing to have made up in the refrigerator. Just buy a bag of the pre-pared coleslaw and pour on this dressing.

2/3 cup vinegar
2/3 cup sugar
2 teaspoons celery seed
1 1/2 teaspoons salt
1/4 teaspoon pepper
1 envelope gelatin, dissolved in
1/2 cup water
2/3 cup salad oil

Combine and bring first six ingredients to a boil. Remove from heat. Add oil and gelatin. Beat well. Store in refrigerator.

COUNTRY CORN BAKE

1 can whole kernel corn
1 can cream style corn
2 eggs
1 carton sour cream
1 small package corn muffin mix
1 stick margarine, melted
1 cup shredded cheddar cheese

Mix all items except margarine and cheese together and place in buttered casserole dish. Pour margarine over top. Bake at 350 degrees for 1/2 hour. Put cheese on top and bake for another 1/2 hour. Let set for a few minutes before serving.

FAVORITE MIXED VEGETABLE CASSEROLE

2 cans mixed vegetables, drained
1 cup onion, chopped
3/4 cup mayonnaise
1 can water chestnuts, chopped
1 cup shredded cheddar cheese
1 cup celery, sliced
1 roll Ritz crackers
Butter

Combine all items except crackers in a casserole dish. Crush crackers and saute in butter. Top casserole with cracker layer, then bake at 350 degrees for 30 minutes.

FROZEN "CANNED" FRUIT SALAD

1 cup mayonnaise
3 small packages cream cheese
2 cups cream, whipped and sweetened
1 cup bananas, chopped fine
1 cup grapes, chopped fine
1 cup crushed pineapple, drained
Walnuts, chopped fine, if desired

Blend the mayonnaise and cream cheese. Stir in fruits and nuts. Fold in cream. Freeze in cans such as soup cans, lined with waxed paper. Before serving, open bottom of can and push out the roll. Slice, if desired.

Freezing popcorn helps eliminate old maids.

ORANGE AND ONION SPINACH SALAD

1 package fresh spinach, torn into bite size pieces
1 Bermuda onion, sliced
2 hard boiled eggs, chopped
1/2 cup bacon bits, optional
1/4 cup oil
2 tablespoons frozen orange juice concentrate, thawed
1 orange, very thinly sliced

Place all items in bowl except oil, orange concentrate, and orange slices. Whip oil and orange juice together. Pour over salad and garnish with the orange slices.

SESAME ALMOND SLAW

1 package slivered almonds
2 tablespoons sesame seed
Butter
2 packages chicken flavor ramen
1 16-ounce package coleslaw
1 small bunch green onion, chopped, including tops
1 cup oil
6 tablespoons rice vinegar
Salt and pepper, if desired

Brown almonds and sesame in butter. In large bowl combine slaw, onions, and noodles from ramen (crush by hand first). Mix oil, vinegar, salt and pepper and one packet of the chicken flavor seasoning packet with the noodles. Add almonds, sesame and dressing to the slaw.

POTLUCK SALAD

1 large carton cottage cheese
1 package orange flavored gelatin, dry
1 large can crushed pineapple, drained
1 large can mandarin oranges, drained
1 cup chopped walnuts
1 large carton frozen whipped topping

Combine all of above ingredients. Makes a large salad ideal to take to a potluck supper. Flavor of gelatin and fruits may be changed, such as strawberry gelatin with strawberries and bananas and pecans, etc.

GARLIC MASHED POTATOES

2 8-ounce russet potatoes
2 cups water
1 1/2 cups chicken broth
3 large garlic cloves (more if desired)
1/2 cup milk
2 tablespoons butter

Peel and cut potatoes into 1-inch pieces. Combine with water, chicken broth and garlic cloves in heavy saucepan. Bring to a boil. Boil uncovered until potatoes are tender and almost all the liquid is absorbed, about 15 minutes. Mash potatoes and garlic. Add milk and butter and mix well. Season with salt and white pepper to taste and serve.

We know Terry Hogan as the "cheesecake man" as he is owner and originator of ***The Original Temptation Co.*** that makes and distributes The Original Sensation Cheesecake Bar. His garlic mashed potatoes recipe is bound to be a treat. He started cooking professionally while living in Essex, CT. He made his way from cooking on the Schooners sailing out of Old Mystic Seaport to Buckley House in New London, CT., to Mexico City and Columbus, Ohio, before coming to the Dakotas.

GREAT CORN OFF THE COB

If you have come about too much corn on the cob, here's an easy and delicious recipe. Cool and freeze any extra.

For each 20 cups cut corn add 1 pound butter and 1 pint half and half cream. Cook in roaster in 325 degree oven for 1 hour.

FRESH CORN SALAD

4 ears cooked corn, cut off the cob
1 small onion, chopped
2 medium cucumbers, sliced
1 cup celery, chopped
2 large tomatoes, chopped

DRESSING:

1 cup sour cream
1 cup mayonnaise
3 tablespoons vinegar
1 teaspoon salt
1 teaspoon sugar
1/4 teaspoon pepper

Combine dressing ingredients and pour over the vegetables. Refrigerate until ready to serve.

GREEN CHILE BAKE

1 can green chiles
1 cup milk
2 eggs
1/4 cup self-rising flour
1 pound Monterey Jack Cheese

Clean out chiles and fill with shredded cheese. Place in small casserole dish. Beat together the milk, eggs and flour and pour over chilies. Top with remaining cheese and bake at 350 degrees for 1/2 hour or until set and done.

My Father tells that many families did not have a place to store potatoes to keep them from freezing, so they cooked them before winter so as to keep them edible. I remember him talking about times being very hard and how they had little except potatoes stored up to eat during one winter season. These were in a storm cellar. The cellar caved in which allowed the potatoes to freeze.

WALDORF SALAD

4-6 apples, chopped with peels on
1 cup celery, sliced
1/2 cup raisins
1/2 cup chopped walnuts

DRESSING:

1/4 cup mayonnaise
1/4 cup non-fat dairy topping
1 teaspoon vanilla

If your apples are large, you may want to increase the amount of the dressing.

ONION PATTIES

2 1/2 cups onion, chopped fine
1 tablespoon dried parsley
3/4 cup flour
1 tablespoon sugar
1 tablespoon cornmeal
2 teaspoons baking powder
2 teaspoons salt
3/4 cup milk

Make batter from all ingredients except parsley and onion, adding them after batter is well blended. Drop from spoon into skillet. Flatten into patties and fry until both sides are golden brown.

One of my most pleasant memories is of visiting my Dad's mother, Bertha. Grandma had a whole yard full of hollyhocks and winter onions. When I see a recipe for onions, I find myself thinking of her taking out her potato fork and digging me a big clump of the onions to take home.

CRANBERRY DELIGHT

2 3-ounce packages gelatin,
cranberry or raspberry
2 cups boiling water
16 ounce can whole cranberry sauce
8 1/4-ounce can crushed pineapple
1/2 cup orange juice
1/4 cup chopped walnuts
Non-dairy whipped topping

Dissolve fruit gelatin in the boiling water. Stir in cranberries, pineapple and orange juice. Chill until starting to set. Stir in walnuts and put the non-dairy whipped topping on top.

MORE FIXIN'S FROM THE GARDEN:

Let's Satisfy Our Sweet Tooth

Vinegar Pie
1000 Oatmeal Raisin Cookies
Mellow Mincemeat Pie
Edith's Buttermilk Raisin Pie
Aunt Annabell's Butterscotch Dessert
Raisin Cookies
Brett's Chocolate Zucchini Cake
Chocolate Peanut Butter Cake
Fresh Apple Cake
Maple Nut Torte
Applesauce Cake
Chocolate Mayonnaise Cake
Sauerkraut Chocolate Cake
Mary Pat's Fry Pan Fudge
Brown Sugar Fudge
Prairie Praline
Pudding Nut Clusters
Chocolate Cream Cheese Fudge
Holiday Divinity
Tomato Soup Bars
Crack Molasses Cookies
Grandma Vaad's Potato Chip Cookies
Loaun's Raisin Bars
Dakota Peanut Butter Cookies
Grandma Star's Lemon Bars
Syrup Brownies
Oatmeal Drops
Sunset on the Prairie Cookies
Orange Slice Candy Cookies
Lemon Lift Cake
Cherries Jubilee
Beef Chocolate Fudge
Beef Candy
Sour Cream Raisin Pie
Lazy Day Brownies
Fast and Simple Fudge
Agnes's Peachy Cake

Gertrude McAnaly was just a wisp of a girl in her mid-twenties when she made the trip alone to the Dakotas in the early 1900's. Her home was in Indiana, and she traveled by train from Chicago to homestead near Dixon, South Dakota, teaching school across the border in Nebraska. One of the items she brought along was a recipe for vinegar pie.

VINEGAR PIE

1 cup sugar
3 tablespoons corn starch
1/2 teaspoon salt
3 eggs
1/4 cup vinegar
2 tablespoons butter
2 cups hot water
1 pre-baked pie shell

Combine sugar, corn starch and salt. Add eggs, vinegar and butter. Stir and add water. Cook until thick, stirring all the time. Pour into pie shell.

Fruit for pies was hard to get in pioneer days. Grandma used this recipe when she homesteaded near Dixon and after marrying another school teacher and settling near Hamill, SD. Their eight children enjoyed desserts like vinegar pie as they grew up in that south central South Dakota community.

WHY FEAR THE DAWN

by Gertrude McAnaly Harless

Why fear the dawn
As time rolls along?
Tho' the whole world is torn apart.
Find solace in work,
From duty ne'er shirk,
And keep peace uppermost in your heart.

Why fear the dawn?
Find rapture in song.
Stand steadfast and firm for the right.
Your victory will be won,
Your battles be done.
You'll rest, where there'll be no more night.

*THE VALLEY TRAIL**

The Valley Trail is a peaceful trail
On the other side of the hill
Where cares and worries
Can never prevail
And pain is forever still.
The Valley Trail is a happy trail
And lovely to think of, too.
For there, in the Light
That Can Never Fail,
Your loved one will wait for you.!

*This was hand written by Grandma Harless. I found it in an atlas, but I don't know if she was the author.

1000 OATMEAL RAISIN COOKIES

15 cups white sugar
16 cups brown sugar
15 1/2 cups shortening
31 eggs
31 cups oatmeal
31 cups flour
30 teaspoons vanilla
11 teaspoons salt
15 teaspoons soda
16 teaspoons baking powder
16 cups raisins

Cream sugar and shortening. Add eggs, beating well. Add oatmeal and other dry ingredients. Stir in vanilla and raisins. Bake on non-stick cookie sheet in moderate oven until edges start to brown.

MELLOW MINCEMEAT PIE

1 package instant vanilla pudding
1 small container frozen whipped topping mix
1/2 cup sour cream
1 cup mincemeat
1 baked pie shell

Make up pudding, reducing liquid by half. Gently stir in remaining ingredients and pour into baked pie shell. Refrigerate to firm. Dollop whipped topping or sweetened sour cream on each piece.

Borax is a good stain remover to use on washable fabrics. Use 1 tablespoon borax in 2 cups water as a soak. If stain is stubborn, apply a borax and water paste. Soak at least 1 hour before washing garment.

EDITH'S BUTTERMILK RAISIN PIE

My favorite pie - except for Mom's apple, lemon, cherry..........

1 1/2 cups raisins
1 cup water
2 eggs
2/3 cup sugar
1 teaspoon vinegar
1 tablespoon cornstarch
1 cup buttermilk
1 baked pie crust shell

Boil raisins in water until tender. Combine all other filling ingredients. Add this to the raisins and cook, stirring constantly until thickened. Pour into the baked shell. Serve with whipped topping.

Reduce oven temperatures by 25 degrees when using glass rather than metal pans.

AUNT ANNABELL'S BUTTERSCOTCH DESSERT

1 can butterscotch pudding
1 yellow cake mix, dry
2 eggs
Topping:
1/3 cup sugar
6 ounces butterscotch chips
1/2 cup nuts

Mix pudding, cake mix and eggs together and put in a jelly roll pan. Put topping on the pudding mixture. Bake at 350 degrees until nicely browned.

Aunt Annabell's cooking was good, really good! I remember it well. Our family would drive to Crookston, Nebraska, then several miles west to spend a few days at that comfortable stone house in the sand hills - and how exciting it was for us to get to visit our four cousins. The table was huge, and it seemed like breakfast lasted forever. Or was everybody lingering so they wouldn't have to help the boys milk cows? How Harley and Jerry hated milking, or at least they had to act like they did!

RAISIN COOKIES

1 cup shortening
1 1/2 cups sugar
3 1/2 cups flour
1 1/2 cups raisins
1 1/2 cups water
2 eggs, well beaten
1 teaspoon soda
1 teaspoon vanilla
1/2 teaspoon salt
1 teaspoon baking powder

Boil raisins in water until all water is absorbed. Cool. Cream shortening and sugar. Add eggs and raisins. Mix in remaining ingredients until well blended. Make into balls and place on non-stick cookie sheet. Press with damp glass dipped in sugar. Bake at 350 degrees 10 to 15 minutes or until lightly browned.

Soak oranges in boiling water for five minutes before peeling. The white membrane will be easily removed.

BRETT'S CHOCOLATE ZUCCHINI CAKE

1 3/4 cups sugar
1/2 cup margarine
1/2 cup oil
2 eggs
1 teaspoon vanilla
1/2 cup buttermilk
2 1/2 cups flour
1/4 cup cocoa
1 teaspoon baking soda
1/2 teaspoon salt
2 1/2 cups grated unpeeled zucchini
1 cup chocolate chips
3/4 cup walnuts
2 tablespoons sugar

Combine sugar, margarine, oil, eggs and vanilla. Beat. Add the remaining ingredients except for chips, nuts and the two tablespoons sugar. Stir. Spread in greased and floured 9x13 pan. Sprinkle the chips, nuts and remaining sugar over the batter. Bake at 325 degrees for 55 minutes. Serve with whipped topping..

CHOCOLATE PEANUT BUTTER CAKE

2 cups sugar
4 eggs
1 cup milk
2 cups flour
1 teaspoon baking powder
1 teaspoon vanilla
1 small jar peanut butter
1/2 pound chocolate bar

Cream sugar and eggs. Add milk, dry ingredients and vanilla and mix well. Bake in greased jelly roll pan at 350 degrees until sides are crusty and pull away. Let cool 3 minutes. Spread with peanut butter. Refrigerate for 10 minutes. Melt candy bar and spread over peanut butter. Cut before chocolate hardens. Store in refrigerator.

I never saw a Purple Cow,
I never hope to see one;
But I can tell you, anyhow,
I'd rather see than be one!
Burgess

FRESH APPLE CAKE

2 eggs
2 cups sugar
1/2 cup oil
1/4 teaspoon salt
2 teaspoons soda
2 teaspoons vanilla
2 teaspoons cinnamon
2 cups plus 2 1/2 tablespoons flour
1 cup chopped nuts
4 cups raw apples, finely diced
1/2 cup brown sugar
2 tablespoons cinnamon
2 tablespoons flour
2 tablespoons melted butter
1/2 cup nuts

Mix eggs, sugar, oil, salt, soda, vanilla, 2 teaspoons cinnamon, flour, 1 cup nuts, and apples together. Pour into greased and floured 9x13 pan. Top with brown sugar, 2 tablespoons cinnamon and flour, butter and 1/2 cup nuts. Bake at 350 degrees for 45 minutes.

MAPLE NUT TORTE

3 egg whites
1 cup sugar
1 teaspoon vanilla
1/2 teaspoon baking powder
16 crumbled soda crackers
1 cup chopped walnuts
8 ounces whipping cream
1 teaspoon maple flavoring
3 tablespoons powdered sugar

Beat egg whites until foamy. Gradually add sugar, beating until stiff. Add vanilla. Fold in remaining ingredients. Pour into well-buttered glass pan (8" square or 9" round works well). Bake in a preheated oven at 325 degrees for 35 minutes. Cool, then top with sweetened whipped cream flavored with the maple flavoring. Whip in powdered sugar to taste. Refrigerate for 4 to 5 hours before serving. This will serve 8 to 9.

This sounds like a *sweetheart of a recipe*. Guess that could be because it comes from a real sweetheart, my Aunt Efe.

APPLESAUCE CAKE

A recipe of Roxy Mooney Bartine passed on to Louise Blum Wagner and then on to the Blum families.

1 1/2 cups applesauce
1 cup boiling water
1 1/2 cups raisins
1/2 cup butter
1 1/2 cups brown sugar
2 eggs
2 1/2 cups flour
1 1/2 teaspoons soda
3/4 teaspoon salt
1 1/2 teaspoons cinnamon
3/4 teaspoon cloves
3/4 teaspoon nutmeg
3/4 cup nuts

Pour boiling water over raisins and set aside. Cream sugar and butter. Add eggs and beat well. Add applesauce. Add dry ingredients to batter. Drain raisins and fold nuts and raisins into batter. Bake in 9x13 pan for 45 minutes at 350 degrees. Cool and frost as desired.

CHOCOLATE MAYONNAISE CAKE

Brenda sent this recipe that belonged to her Mom. No shortening or eggs in this recipe --wish I'd have thought of that!

2 cups flour
1 cup sugar
4 tablespoons cocoa
1 teaspoon baking powder
1 teaspoon soda
1 cup mayonnaise
1 cup cold water
1 teaspoon vanilla

Sift together flour, sugar, cocoa, baking powder and soda. Add mayonnaise, cold water and vanilla. Beat two minutes. Bake in 2 9" layer pans or one 11x13 at 350 degrees for 30-35 minutes.

Bread and milk poultices work on slivers and small infected areas. Trust me--they do work!

SAUERKRAUT CHOCOLATE CAKE

Tracy collected recipes during her year of travels with Up With People.

2/3 cup butter
1 3/8 cups sugar
3 eggs
1 teaspoon vanilla
1/2 cup cocoa
2 1/4 cups flour
1 teaspoon baking powder
1/4 teaspoon salt
3/4 teaspoon soda
1 1/4 cups water
2/3 cup sauerkraut (rinse, drain and chop)

Cream butter and sugar. Beat in eggs and vanilla. Add sifted dry ingredients alternately with water. Stir in sauerkraut. Turn batter into two greased and floured 8" pans. Bake 30 minutes at 350 degrees. Use your favorite frosting or dust with powdered sugar.

MARY PAT'S FRY PAN FUDGE

Cook this fudge in your heaviest fry pan!

2 cups sugar
3 tablespoons butter
1 cup evaporated milk
1/2 teaspoon salt
8 diced marshmallows
1 large package chocolate chips
1 cup nuts
1 teaspoon vanilla

Combine sugar, salt, butter and milk in fry pan. Set controls at 280 degrees. Bring to a boil. Stir with wooden spoon. After boiling for 5 minutes, shut off heat. Add chips and marshmallows. Stir vigorously until well blended. Add vanilla and nuts. Pour into buttered pan and cut.

The advantage of doing one's praising for oneself is that one can lay it on so thick and exactly in the right places. *Butler*

BROWN SUGAR FUDGE

2 cups brown sugar, packed
1 cup white sugar
1/2 cup white syrup
1 1/2 cups milk
2 tablespoons butter
2 or 3 drops maple extract
1 cup walnut pieces

Cook the sugars, syrup and milk together. This will take approximately 20 to 25 minutes cooking time to reach the stage where it coats the spoon. Add butter and maple extract. Beat until smooth. Add walnuts and stir.

Coughs were a "nagging" problem on the prairies. Many cough syrup formulas were tried - some seemed to fit the kill or cure category! This one doesn't sound too bad: Mix together equal parts of lemon juice, honey, olive oil and glycerine.

PRAIRIE PRALINES

A favorite if you're a pecan lover!

2 cups white sugar
3/4 teaspoon soda
1 cup light cream (half & half)
1 1/2 tablespoons butter
2 cups pecans

Combine sugar, soda and cream in large, heavy pan. Bring to boil over medium heat, stirring constantly. Reduce heat and cook, stirring, to soft ball stage. Mixture will caramelize slightly. Remove from heat and add butter. Stir in pecans and beat until thick (2-3 minutes). Mixture will look dark and shiny. Drop by teaspoons onto waxed paper. If it becomes too thick, add 1 tablespoon hot water while beating. Makes 30 candies.

Store nuts in the freezer, including the nuts with shells still on them. They will come out of the shell easier if cracked while frozen.

PUDDING NUT CLUSTERS

1 package chocolate pudding mix (not instant)
1 cup sugar
1/2 cup evaporated milk
1 tablespoon butter or margarine
1 cup small salted peanuts

Mix all ingredients except peanuts together in a heavy 1 1/2 quart saucepan. Cook and stir to full over-all boil. Lower heat and keep stirring while mixture boils slowly for 3 minutes. Take off heat. Stir in peanuts all at once. Beat until candy starts to thicken. Drop from teaspoon onto waxed paper.

This recipe works with any flavor of pudding and nuts of your choice.

Adversity is sometimes hard upon a man; but for one man who can stand prosperity, there are a hundred that will stand adversity.
Carlyle

CHOCOLATE CREAM CHEESE FUDGE

4 cups powdered sugar
8 ounce package cream cheese
4 1-ounce squares unsweetened chocolate, melted
1 teaspoon vanilla
Dash of salt
1/2 cup chopped nuts

Gradually add sugar to softened cream cheese, mixing until well blended. Stir in remaining ingredients. Spread in buttered 8-inch square pan. Chill for several hours or overnight. Makes 1 3/4 pounds of fabulous fudge.

Remove coffee and tea stains from cups by rubbing with a baking powder paste.

HOLIDAY DIVINITY

A true no fail divinity recipe!

3 cups sugar
3/4 cup light corn syrup
3/4 cup hot water
1/4 teaspoon salt
2 egg whites
1 small package gelatin
1 cup chopped nuts
1/2 cup coconut, optional

Cook sugar, corn syrup, water and salt, stirring constantly until sugar dissolves. Cook to hard boil stage without stirring. Remove from heat. While the syrup is cooking, beat the egg whites until soft peaks form. Gradually beat in either red or green gelatin. Beat until stiff peaks form. Pour hot syrup slowly over egg white mixture, beating constantly at high speed until soft peaks form. Stir in nuts and coconut. Drop from teaspoon on waxed paper.

Does your soup taste too salty? Cut up a potato into several pieces and place in the soup. Discard these pieces as they will have absorbed some of the salt.

While you're making the Holiday Divinity, you may enjoy reading the following letter written by my daughter when she was in grade school. You can tell from some of the items she wanted in her stocking that she liked to cook even at that young age!

Dear Santa Claus,

I would like a tape player or a recorder, a pizza maker and a basketball, an alarm clock and maybe a new pair of ice skates for later. Also the game Jaws and Pokeno.

I wish I had my old watch that I lost or a new one like it. Someday I'd like a mini-bike; even now, maybe. Maybe a bee-bee gun for in the summer.

In my stocking I would like a package of Philadelphia cream cheese and some other things like film for my camera, a pair of gloves to feed with, a package of banana bread, new cards, and tapes for the tape player or just tape for the recorder.

If you would like cookies, they are in containers on the table.

I'd like a gumball machine or someday a telephone in my room, a pocket fisherman and, for our family, a snow mobile for some day.

Love Tracy Vaad

Merry Christmas, Merry Xmas, Santa Claus

TOMATO SOUP BARS

1 1/2 cups flour
1 teaspoon baking powder
1/2 teaspoon soda
2 teaspoons cinnamon
1 teaspoon allspice
1 can tomato soup
1 1/3 cups brown sugar
2 eggs
1/2 cup vegetable oil
1 cup rolled oats
1 cup nuts, chips or raisins

Combine flour, baking powder, soda and spices. Add soup, sugar, eggs and oil. Beat several minutes. Stir in rolled oats and nuts. Spread in a greased 10x15 pan. Bake at 350 degrees for 25 minutes and frost if desired.

Remove both ends of cans such as tuna comes in and use as molds when poaching eggs.

CRACK MOLASSES COOKIES

A good friend of Grandma Harless gave us this recipe many years ago. I enjoyed typing it from her original handwritten sheet.

4 cups sugar
1 1/2 cups shortening
2 eggs
8 tablespoons mild molasses
1 1/2 teaspoons salt
2 teaspoons cinnamon
2 teaspoons ginger
5 level teaspoons soda
4 cups flour

Cream sugar and shortening. Beat in eggs and molasses, then all dry ingredients. Chill. Make into teaspoon size balls and roll each in sugar. These will flatten when baked. They bake quickly and are hard and crisp. Put into tightly covered container with a couple of slices of bread to soften. This recipe makes 90 to 110 cookies. Bake at 375 degrees. I would recommend a non-stick cookie sheet whenever you bake cookies.

GRANDMA VAAD'S POTATO CHIP COOKIES

I've seen other potato chip cookie recipes, but this one is so simple and so delicious!

1 stick margarine
1/4 cup sugar
1/2 cup finely crushed chips
1 teaspoon vanilla
1 cup flour

Mix thoroughly. Drop by spoonfuls on cookie sheet and press flat with a fork dipped in sugar. Bake approximately 10 minutes at 375 degrees.

Little deeds of kindness, little words of love, help to make earth happy, like the heaven above. *Carney*

LOAUN'S RAISIN BARS

If you have raisin fans in the family, this will be a favorite.

2 cups raisins
3 tablespoons flour
3/4 cup sugar
1 cup water
2 cups flour
1 1/4 cups brown sugar
2 cups quick oatmeal
1 1/2 teaspoons soda
1 1/4 cups margarine

Boil raisins, first flour, sugar and water until thick. Mix second flour with brown sugar, oatmeal and soda. Add melted margarine and mix until crumbly. Put 1/2 crumb mixture in pan. Cover with filling, and put remaining crumb mixture on top. Bake 20 to 30 minutes at 325 degrees.

Out where the handclasp's a little stronger, Out where the smile dwells a little longer, That's where the West begins. Chapman

DAKOTA PEANUT BUTTER COOKIES

This recipe makes a large batch of cookies. Use your favorite oil for shortening.

1 cup oil
1 cup peanut butter
1 cup white sugar
1 cup brown sugar
2 eggs
1 teaspoon vanilla
2 1/2 cups flour
1 1/2 teaspoons soda
1 cup salted peanuts

Mix oil and peanut butter well. Add sugars and eggs and beat. Stir in remaining ingredients. Bake eight minutes at 375 degrees. Use a non-stick cookie sheet.

Try this tip - cheese will grate easily if very cold.

GRANDMA STAR'S ABSOLUTELY EASIEST LEMON BARS YOU'VE EVER MADE

Linda shared her Grandma Star's recipe, and she's right - unbelievably easy!

1 can lemon pie filling
1 box 1-step angel food cake mix

Mix angel food cake mix powder and lemon pie filling together. Pour onto deep cookie sheet or bar pan. Bake at 350 degrees for 15 to 20 minutes. Dust with powdered sugar or spread a thin glaze of powdered sugar and lemon juice if desired.

The centipede was happy quite, until the toad in fun, said "Pray which leg goes after which?" And worked her mind to such a pitch, she lay distracted in the ditch, considering how to run. Craster

SYRUP BROWNIES

Many years ago when we were visiting Travis's Godmother, she served these brownies. I thought they were the best I had ever eaten.

1 cup sugar
1 stick margarine
4 eggs
1 large can chocolate syrup
1 cup flour
1/2 cup chopped nuts
Pinch of salt

Cream sugar and margarine. Add eggs and beat. Mix in remaining ingredients. Pour into large cake pan that you have greased and floured. Bake 25 minutes at 350 degrees. Frost with chocolate frosting.

If a recipe calls for sour milk, use 1 cup sweet milk to which you add 1 tablespoon lemon juice or vinegar or 1 3/4 teaspoons cream of tartar.

OATMEAL DROPS

You'll get lots of requests for this recipe anytime you serve these cookies!

1 cup raisins
1/2 cup hot water
2 cups flour
1 teaspoon soda
1 teaspoon salt
1 teaspoon nutmeg
1 teaspoon cinnamon
2 cups oatmeal
1 cup brown sugar
1/2 cup chopped nuts
2 eggs
3/4 cup salad oil
1 teaspoon vanilla

Soak raisins in hot water and set aside. Sift flour with next four ingredients. Add oatmeal, brown sugar and nuts to dry mixture and blend. In small bowl beat eggs with fork. Add salad oil, vanilla and undrained raisins. Pour into dry mixture, and stir until well blended. Drop by teaspoons on ungreased cookie sheet. Bake at 350 degrees 10 to 13 minutes. These are good when you use 1/2 cup golden and 1/2 cup regular raisins.

SUNSET ON THE PRAIRIE COOKIES

3/4 cup shortening (part butter or margarine will work)
1/2 cup sugar
1 small package fruit flavored gelatin
2 eggs
1 teaspoon vanilla
2 1/2 cups flour
1 teaspoon baking powder
1 teaspoon salt

Cream shortening, sugar and gelatin. Add eggs and vanilla. Stir in dry ingredients. Shape into one inch balls and place on ungreased baking sheet. Flatten with glass dipped in sugar. Bake at 400 degrees for 6 to 8 minutes.

We plough the field, and scatter
The good seed on the land,
But it is fed and watered
By God's Almighty Hand.
He sends the snow in winter,
The warmth to swell the grain,
The breezes and the sunshine,
And soft refreshing rain.
Campbell

ORANGE SLICE CANDY COOKIES

1 cup shortening
2 cups brown sugar
3 eggs
3 1/2 cups flour
1 teaspoon cream of tartar
1 teaspoon soda
18 orange slice candies, chopped
1/2 cup walnuts

Dredge orange slices in 1/2 cup of the flour and set aside. Cream shortening and sugar. Add eggs and beat. Add dry ingredients, blending well. Stir in orange slices and walnuts. Make into balls, roll in sugar and press down with fork. Bake at 350 degrees until a delicate light brown.

The Twelve Months
Snowy, Flowy, Blowy
Showery, Flowery, Bowery
Hoppy, Croppy, Droppy
Breezy, Sneezy, Freezy

Sir Gregory Gander

LEMON LIFT CAKE

1 package lemon cake mix
4 eggs
1 package lemon flavored gelatin
3/4 cup water
3/4 cup vegetable oil

Topping:
2 cups sifted powdered sugar
Juice and rind of 2 lemons

Combine all cake ingredients and beat with mixer for 4 minutes. Pour into greased 9x13 cake pan. Bake at 350 degrees for 35 to 40 minutes. Remove cake from oven and punch holes over-all with fork.

Mix and stir topping ingredients until well blended. Pour over top of cake while still hot. Let cool. Serve as is or with whipped cream or ice cream. Serves 12-16.

How pleased I am to get this recipe from my cousin. When her family would come from California to visit us, she would ride our reliable old horse, Polly. It wasn't a problem getting her on as she was so tiny, but sure was to get her off - she loved that horse!

CHERRIES JUBILEE

Bing cherries
Butter
Brown sugar
1 orange
Kirsch (cherry liqueur)
Brandy

Cook cherries with butter, brown sugar, juice of the orange and the Kirsch until thickened. Cut the rind of the orange into a long spiral piece and add to the pan. Pour in brandy. Pick up some of the brandy in a spoon and light. Pour this over the orange rind spiral and it will flame and light the rest of the dessert. Serve over vanilla ice cream.

This wonderful sounding recipe is shared by Timothy Burrell. He has worked in food and beverage at hotels and country clubs for 24 years. My Aunt Della was visiting us here in South Dakota. We were eating at a local restaurant, and she asked if they had cherries jubilee. They didn't! I hope Tim will make this next time she comes.

My Father's brother, John, suffered from diabetes during his childhood and died from the disease right before the discovery of insulin. Dad marvels at how brave he was and how optimistic he was that there would be a cure for the disease. John wrote for information on miracle cures when he would find advertisements in magazines or papers. This is a pamphlet he received in the mail during December 1924.

What Others Say About "BETO"

A Blessing to Diabetics

JOHN BARING
736 N. Lotus Ave., CHICAGO, ILL.

Tornado season is a scary time on the prairies. Mom speaks of her brother being out in a field when one hit, and he hung onto our "tough" prairie grasses as it tossed him around. This is a letter written by Dad's brother, John, on June 15, 1924, from Lower Brule, SD, after a tornado had hit.

Dear Mother and all:

Well how was the storm down there. It was sure a bad one here. I was alone. Papa was up in the bend.

It blew the house over and broke it all up, and it hit the corner of the tent when it went and the tent is all in rags. The house hit the chicken coop and knocked it flat on the ground. It killed the hen duck that I got from Dwyers. I had three hens setting with duck eggs in the coop and spoiled all of the eggs. The eggs in the incubators were about half good, but it upset when the tent went down. They were just pecking the shells.

I have 14 little chickens and I saved them all through the storm. Just as soon as I saw that the cyclone was coming, I ran for the cave. There were pieces of the house about three quarters of a mile from here. You know that big long building right there by the store. It blew flat to the ground and lots of other things. Our 2 oil stoves blew away, too. It did a lot of damage............Love, John

P.S. That church that Mr. DeBrays preaches in blew flat to the ground. I tell you it was a bad one. We lost about $250.00 worth of stuff.

BEEF CHOCOLATE FUDGE

Yes, you read the name right. This makes wonderful "old fashioned" style fudge.

2 cups white sugar
1 cup brown sugar
1/2 white corn syrup
1/2 cup milk
1 teaspoon vanilla
1/2 cup ground roast beef or cooked ground beef
3 tablespoons butter
2 ounces unsweetened chocolate
1/2 cup chopped walnuts

Cook all together in a heavy pan to soft ball (238 degrees) without stirring. Remove from heat and let cool to lukewarm. Beat until thick.

BEEF CANDY

Another unusual recipe for those who may not want a chocolate candy.

2 cups white sugar
1 cup brown sugar
1/2 cup corn syrup
3 tablespoons butter
1/2 cup milk
1/2 cup ground beef, cooked
1 teaspoon vanilla
1/2 cup chopped nuts
1/2 cup coconut

Combine all ingredients except vanilla, nuts and coconut. Cook to firm ball stage. Let cool to 120 degrees. Beat until creamy. Add vanilla, nuts and coconut. Pour into buttered pan.

Wet newspapers laid over oil spill will usually absorb the oil by the time the newspapers are dry.

SOUR CREAM RAISIN PIE

1 baked pie crust (9" or 10")
1 1/2 cups raisins
1/2 cup water
1/2 cup sour cream
1/2 teaspoon cinnamon
1/2 teaspoon instant coffee
Dash of ground cloves
4 ounce box regular vanilla pudding
2 cups milk
2 egg yolks

Simmer raisins in the water. Steam in covered pan for 10 minutes. Remove from heat but do not drain. Stir in sour cream, cinnamon, instant coffee and cloves. Let cool slightly while you prepare the pudding. Prepare the pudding according to instructions on box with 2 cups of milk. When thick add the egg yolks. Cook until smooth and thick. Use double boiler for best results. Stir raisin and sour cream mixture into pudding and fill crust.

3 egg whites
1 teaspoon vanilla
1/2 cup sugar
1 teaspoon cream of tartar

Prepare meringue by beating egg whites to soft peaks. Gradually add the remaining ingredients and beat until stiff. Top pie filling, spreading to the edge. Brown in 350 degree oven.

The Sour Cream Raisin Pie recipe was developed by Bro. David Nagel a member of the Congregation of the Priests of the Sacred Heart. For 11 years Bro. David was the Food Service Director at St. Joseph's Indian School and for the last five years has served as Director of Development. The recipe has received national recognition by a professional food service magazine as an outstanding dessert idea.

LAZY DAY BROWNIES

1 cup butter, melted
4 tablespoons cocoa
2 cups sugar
4 eggs
1 1/3 cups flour
2 teaspoons vanilla
1/2 teaspoon salt
1 cup nuts, chopped

Blend all of the ingredients. Put into a 9x13 non-stick pan. Bake at 350 degrees for 30-40 minutes.

FAST N' SIMPLE FUDGE

A great recipe from my cousin, Stephanie. She says it doubles very easily, and she tries to keep the ingredients on hand for when she needs a quick dessert.

1 pound box powdered sugar
1 egg
1 teaspoon vanilla
1 cube margarine
4 ounces unsweetened baking chocolate squares
Pinch of salt
1/4 cup low fat milk

Mix powdered sugar and salt; slowly fork in egg and what is needed of milk and vanilla. Mixture will be very thick like putty. Melt chocolate and butter in double boiler or microwave for 1 1/2 minutes to 2 minutes depending on micro-power. Fork the hot mixture into the powdered sugar mixture, stirring in until chocolate mixture is even in color. Stir in nuts. Place in 8x8 buttered dish (9x13 pan if doubled). Chill until firm. Cut in 1 inch pieces. Makes 64 pieces.

AGNES'S PEACHY CAKE

1/2 cup butter or margarine
1/2 cup sugar
1 teaspoon grated lemon rind
2 eggs
1 cup flour
1 teaspoon baking powder
1/4 teaspoon salt
4 peaches, sliced
1/3 cup sugar
1/4 teaspoon cinnamon

Cream the butter with sugar. Add the lemon rind, if desired. Beat in the eggs, one at a time. Sift the flour, baking powder and salt together. Slowly beat into the batter. Pour 1/2 of batter into a greased 8x8 pan. Cover with the sliced peaches. Combine second sugar and the cinnamon and sprinkle on top. Pour other half of batter over top. Bake at 350 degrees for 50 minutes. Serve with whipped cream or ice cream.

MORE SWEET TOOTH RECIPES:

Whet Your Appetite -- Wet Your Whistle

Chili Dip
Cheese Sticks
Cheese Spread
Colada Punch
Hot Mulled Cider
Frozen Slush Punch
Wine Punch
Cheese Puffs
Mom's Egg & Cheese Sandwich Spread
Frosty Orange Drink
Frosty Grape Drink
Homemade Cappucino
Jazebell Sauce
Rhubarb Slush
Fruit Dip
Mexican Appetizer
Honey Of A Fruit Dip
Punch With A Punch
South Of The Border Appeteasers
Pickled Eggs
Cauliflower Fritters
Chocolate Banana Shake

CHILI DIP

A hot dip for a cold night on the prairies. Makes enough to take to a barn dance!

3 8-ounce packages cream cheese
1 cup sharp cheddar cheese, shredded
3 15 1/2-ounce cans chili without beans
6 to 9 drops hot sauce

In large saucepan mix cheese and chili. Add cheese and hot sauce. Heat slowly to simmering, stirring occasionally. Serve hot with corn chips.

Flavor oil used in salad dressings by putting garlic cloves in the bottle.

CHEESE STICKS

Pie pastry for 1 crust
1 cup grated processed cheese
1 teaspoon salt

Roll pastry to 1/8 inch thickness. Sprinkle half of the cheese and salt on half of the pastry. Fold pastry over then fold again four times. Roll out pastry. Repeat above instructions. After final folding, roll to 1/4 inch thickness. Cut in strips. Bake on greased baking sheet in 400 degree oven 8 to 10 minutes. This should make about 3 dozen sticks.

Need to loosen or tighten an item? Remember this formula--lefty loosy, righty tighty!

CHEESE SPREAD

If you have kids in the house, you'll no doubt find the jar of cheese spread in the refrigerator EMPTY! Try this recipe to make your own.

1 pound processed cheese food
1/3 cup milk
1/4 teaspoon onion salt
1/4 teaspoon celery salt
1/4 teaspoon garlic salt
1 stick margarine

Place all ingredients in double boiler. Heat and stir until all is melted and is smooth and creamy. Put in jar while hot. Refrigerate.

COLADA PUNCH

1 15-ounce can cream of coconut
2 ounces white creme de menthe
1 cup white rum
1 cup heavy cream
Ginger ale

Place all items except ginger ale in blender. Blend until frothy. Pour in large punch bowl. Add a bottle of ginger ale until foam bubbles. If desired, sprinkle cinnamon or nutmeg on the top.

After oiling your sewing machine, stitch through a blotter several times.

HOT MULLED CIDER

2 quarts apple cider
1/4 cup brown sugar
1/4 cup white sugar
4 sticks cinnamon
1 teaspoon whole cloves
1 orange, sliced

Cook in slow cooker or on low heat in oven for several hours before serving. This will serve around 12 guests.

Good sunburn remedies - apply apple cider vinegar or a paste of soda and water.

FROZEN SLUSH PUNCH

2 12-ounce cans frozen orange juice
2 12-ounce cans frozen lemonade
1 large can pineapple juice
1 quart ginger ale
5 bananas
4 cups sugar
6 cups water

Boil sugar and water. Cool. Put bananas in blender. Mix all ingredients and freeze.

When you clean your varnished wood, use a cloth dampened in cold tea.

WINE PUNCH

4 cups water
2 cups powdered sugar
1 each orange, lemon and lime
Red wine

Bring water and sugar to a boil and simmer for several minutes. Slice fruit and add to syrup and let set for an hour. Fill large container with ice cubes and add syrup, fruit and wine until it tastes just right to you. This is sometimes called sangria.

To brighten your carpets, sprinkle generously with salt before you vacuum.

CHEESE PUFFS

24 bread rounds
4 tablespoons Parmesan cheese
1/2 cup mayonnaise
1 package onion dip mix
2 egg whites, stiffly beaten

Toast the bread rounds under broiler on one side only. Mix together remaining ingredients. Spoon onto the untoasted side of rounds. Bake 10 minutes at 450 degrees.

Greasy gravy??? Add a little baking soda!!!

MOM'S CHEESE & EGG SANDWICH SPREAD

1/2 pound processed cheese
3 hard boiled eggs
1 tablespoon ground onion
1 tablespoon pimento
1 tablespoon sugar
1 tablespoon vinegar
Salad dressing

Grind or mash cheese and hard boiled eggs. Add onion, pimento, sugar and vinegar. Use just enough salad dressing to make it right for spreading.

I remember getting these ready for card parties when I was young. We would use the little rye bread slices for mini open-faced sandwiches. After spreading them with the cheese and egg spread, we decorated them with slices of stuffed green olives.

FROSTY ORANGE DRINK

If you like to have an orange julius while shopping in the mall, you'll love this recipe.

1 can frozen orange juice
1 cup milk
1 cup water
1/2 teaspoon vanilla
1 tablespoon sugar
12 ice cubes

Combine in blender until smooth. Serve immediately. This is a favorite of the students enrolled in home economics classes at St. Joseph's Indian School. Thank you to them and their instructor for sharing this recipe with us.

Line the crisper section of your refrigerator with newspapers - change every week to keep fresh.

FROSTY GRAPE DRINK

Prefer grape? Try this for a change.

1 can frozen grape juice
1 cup milk
1 cup water
1/2 teaspoon vanilla
12 ice cubes

Prepare like Frosty Orange Drink on the previous page. Enjoy!

HOMEMADE CAPPUCCINO

1 cup brewed coffee
2 heaping teaspoons hot cocoa mix
1 heaping teaspoon non-dairy creamer

Make sure the coffee is very hot. Stir vigorously or use an electric drink stirrer or blender. Add flavoring extracts if desired.

The past is something to profit from, not something to dwell on.

JAZEBELL SAUCE

5 ounce jar prepared horseradish
12 ounce can dry mustard
18 ounce jar pineapple preserves
18 ounce jar apple jelly
1 teaspoon coarse ground pepper

Mix horseradish and mustard; add the rest of the ingredients. This keeps for months in the refrigerator. It makes a good side dish with ham or pour it over cream cheese to use as a dip with crackers. Makes a very large batch!

This is a recipe Kay Andera has included in her cookbook, *I Love Recipes*. Jazebell Sauce is a recipe from her husband, Leonard. Thanks, Kay, for letting us share this recipe in our book, too.

RHUBARB SLUSH

3 cups chopped fresh or frozen rhubarb
1 cup water
1/3 cup sugar
1 cup apple juice
6 ounces frozen pink lemonade concentrate, thawed
2 liter bottle lemon-lime soda

Combine rhubarb, water and sugar and bring to a boil. Reduce heat, cover and simmer for 5 minutes or until tender. Cool for approximately 30 minutes. Puree mixture. Stir in apple juice and lemonade. Pour into a freezer container, cover and freeze until firm. Remove from freezer 45 minutes before needed. Place in punch bowl, add soda and stir.

Save your egg cartons. Put lint from your drier in each compartment. Pour wax over lint to make little starters for your camping fires.

FRUIT DIP

It's a peach of a dip!

12 or 16 ounce container non-dairy whipped topping
1 box custard flavored pudding
2 ounces peach schnapps

Mix until thick. Serve with your favorite fruits.

One of the stores in Lower Brule in the 1930's was owned by my Father and his Dad. An Indian man who lived about three miles north of Lower Brule came into the store and wanted to echasna (charge) some groceries, claiming he would bring in a coyote hide to pay for them. When asked why he didn't bring the hide with him, Peter said he hadn't caught it yet! Lots of bartering was done in those days.

MEXICAN APPETIZER

8 ounces sour cream
8 ounces cream cheese
1/2 packet of taco seasoning

Blend ingredients well and spread on serving dish. Cover with layers of topping such as shredded lettuce, onions, tomatoes, shredded cheese, black olives, avocados, chilies, etc. Serve with taco chips and crackers for dipping.

Love one only, make friends of many, spread goodwill to all.

HONEY OF A FRUIT DIP

2 tablespoons honey
1 cup yogurt
1 cup cream cheese
1/2 teaspoon vanilla

Soften cream cheese. Add balance of ingredients and blend well. Refrigerate until ready to serve with fruits such as strawberries, melon and apples.

Another use for egg cartons: store flower bulbs in them over the winter. Punch holes to allow air to circulate.

PUNCH WITH A PUNCH

1 can frozen cranberry juice
1 can frozen lemonade
Club soda

Thaw cans of concentrate just until slushy. Place in punch bowl. Stir in club soda until the desired strength. This is quite "bitey" and should be served in small glasses.

If you have a milk allergy and need to drink soybean milk, you may have found it doesn't taste real desirable. If so, heat raisins in apple juice. Let this cool. Blend in some honey or sugar and the soybean powder with some additional water.

SOUTH OF THE BORDER APPETEASERS

1 cup cream cheese
1 cup sour cream
1/4 packet taco seasoning
1 can diced chilies
1 can diced black olives
1 cup shredded cheese
Four tortillas

Combine above ingredients except for tortillas. Spread the filling on the tortillas and roll tightly. Chill these well. Slice when ready to serve.

PICKLED EGGS

6 hard boiled eggs, peeled
1 cup vinegar
Juice from 1 can beets
1/2 teaspoon seasoning salt

Place eggs in a quart jar. Bring vinegar, beet juice and seasoning salt to a boil and pour over eggs. These turn out real pretty and can be used to decorate relish trays.

If you sling mud, your hands are going to get dirty!

CAULIFLOWER FRITTERS

1 pound cauliflower, broken into flowerets
1 egg
3/4 cup milk
3/4 cup flour
1 teaspoon sugar
3/4 teaspoon baking powder
1/4 teaspoon salt
Pinch of nutmeg

Cook cauliflower 6 to 7 minutes. While it cooks, beat egg with milk. Combine dry ingredients and gradually stir into the milk mixture. Beat until smooth. Dip cauliflower and fry in hot fat until brown.

A friend is one who knows you and likes you anyway!

CHOCOLATE BANANA SHAKE

3/4 cup milk
3 tablespoons chocolate malt powder
1 banana
2 1/2 to 3 cups ice cream

Blend well. This is a recipe my nephew, Mark, likes to make. He suggests you might want to substitute strawberries, peaches or oreo cookies for the banana and vanilla malt powder for the chocolate. And he ought to know!

I thought it was a joke when my Dad mentioned having used skunk oil on his chest for a cold remedy. He told me that a skunk has a layer of fat under the skin. His mother would remove this and render the fat for the oil - for medicinal purposes!

MORE APPETIZERS:

MORE BEVERAGES:

Recipes from the Good Old Days

Suet Pudding
Mincemeat
Homemade Sandwich Spread
Quick and Easy Sweet Pickles
Dill Pickles
Beet Pickles
Chokecherry Jelly
Chokecherry Syrup
Chokecherry Wine
Grandma Hall's Mustard
Refrigerator Pickles
Green Tomato Pie
Dandelion Jelly
Lambsquarters Greens
Mustard Pickles
Whipped Cream Krumkake

SUET PUDDING

1 cup suet, cut fine
1 cup molasses
1 cup milk
3 cups flour
1 teaspoon soda
1/2 cup raisins
1/2 cup currants
1 1/2 teaspoons salt
1/2 teaspoon ginger
1/2 teaspoon cloves
1/2 teaspoon nutmeg
1 teaspoon cinnamon

Mix all ingredients together and put into glass or metal containers (makes three one-pound coffee tins). Steam this for three hours. You may want to serve this with a rum or vanilla sauce.

Soaking balloons in hot water makes them easier to blow up.

MINCEMEAT

Jeanne's recipe for homemade mincemeat.

3 pounds meat
1/2 pound suet or 1/2 pound butter
2 1/2 quarts apples, peeled and chopped
2 pounds raisins, 1/2 white, 1/2 dark
2 pounds dried currants
1/4 pound citron, diced, optional
2 tablespoons orange peel, chopped fine
2 cups sugar
2 teaspoons salt
4 teaspoons cinnamon
2 teaspoons nutmeg
2 teaspoons allspice
1 1/2 teaspoons cloves
2 cups apple cider
2 cups pineapple juice
3/4 cup vinegar
1/4 cup butter
Rind of 1 lemon, grated
Juice of 1 lemon
2 cups white corn syrup

Cook meat in water. Grind or chop fine. Cook stock down to 3/4 cup. If you are using hamburger, leave out suet. Grind suet fine or melt butter. Combine meat, suet and apples. Add raisins, currants, citron, orange and lemon. Heat to boiling. Add remaining ingredients and heat again. This may be frozen. It will make eight pies. Be sure to use a large (2 gallon) kettle when cooking the mincemeat.

HOMEMADE SANDWICH SPREAD

1 cup green tomatoes
1 cup carrots
1 cup cucumbers
1 cup green peppers
1 cup red peppers
1 cup onion
1 cup water

DRESSING

3 tablespoons flour
2 tablespoons dry mustard
1 teaspoon salt
3 tablespoons butter
2 egg yolks
1/2 cup sugar
1/2 cup water
1/2 cup vinegar

Grind vegetables before measuring 1 cup of each. Add the water and cook until tender. Drain. Cook dressing until it thickens. Mix with vegetables. Seal in hot sterilized jars. Process in a boiling water bath.

QUICK AND EASY SWEET PICKLES

Wash and firmly pack 4 inch or smaller cukes into sterilized quart jar. To each quart add one scant teaspoon alum, one tablespoon canning salt, one teaspoon mixed pickling spice (Mom uses dill instead) and one cup vinegar. Finish filling the jar with cold water. Put on seal and shake to dissolve. Do not heat. Put in a cool, dry, dark place and leave at least 3 weeks. When you want to use (not before), drain and wash the cukes well. Slice in half lengthwise and sprinkle with 1 cup sugar (or more for crisper pickles). Refrigerate for 24 hours, shaking occasionally. Enjoy - is that easy or what!

DILL PICKLES

Everybody has a special method for making dill pickles. Our formula is 1-3-9, meaning 1 cup salt, 3 cups vinegar and 9 cups water. Pour this solution hot into jars packed with the cucumbers, 1/4 teaspoon alum and 1 clove of garlic plus lots of dill. (Dad loves dill and it seems like he always comments "It could have used more dill"!) If in a hurry, I just turn the jar upside down after sealing with sterilized jar lids. But if you want to be sure they seal, bring to a boil in a boiling water bath cooker. Then just turn off the heat and let cool.

BEET PICKLES

If you raise beets in the garden, you need to go through the process of boiling them until tender, slipping off the skins and packing in the jars. Small beets can be pickled whole while larger ones should be chunked or sliced. If fresh beets aren't available, you can drain canned beets and proceed with the pickling.

BEET PICKLING SOLUTION

2 cups vinegar
2 cups brown sugar
1 teaspoon salt
2 tablespoons pickling spices

I feel most comfortable putting these in a boiling water bath to be sure they seal.

CHOKECHERRIES, OUR PRAIRIE FRUIT

Have you ever picked one of those burgundy colored berries - they look so delicious and taste good. But the strange sensation in your mouth will give you a clue as to how they got their name!

CHOKECHERRY JELLY

As if the picking isn't enough, now the real work begins. And caution must be taken while working with these prairie berries as they do stain everything - pans, stove top, counter, floor, dish cloth, etc.

Rinse off berries. Place in LARGE pan, covering with water. Cook until fruit will fall away from seed easily. You will need to put the berries and liquid through a colander (then strain through cheesecloth if you want a clear jelly). Cook this using a pectin recipe for berries and seal in hot jars using sterilized lids. Turn the jars over and stand on their tops until sealed.

CHOKECHERRY SYRUP

We never mean to make syrup - it just happens. So plan on enjoying chokecherry syrup on your pancakes and french toast if you make chokecherry jelly very often. For some unknown reason it sometimes will not set up. Chokecherry syrup - it just happens!

You can use the same proportions of sugar and fruit suggested in the pectin recipe, leaving out the pectin and simmering until the consistency you like.

CHOKECHERRY WINE

For each gallon juice use 3 pounds sugar. Heat a small amount of the juice and stir in sugar. Pour with the rest of juice into a stone crock. For each 5 gallons of liquid, add 3/4 of a yeast cake. Stir with a wooden spoon. Skim each day until it no longer "works". Store covered in glass jugs.

GRANDMA HALL'S MUSTARD

6 tablespoons dry mustard
6 tablespoons flour
1 tablespoon sugar
1 teaspoon salt
1/4 teaspoon red pepper
1/4 teaspoon black pepper
1 cup vinegar
2 cups water
3 eggs

Mix together dry ingredients. Beat eggs and mix in. Bring water and vinegar to a boil and mix dry ingredients and eggs into this. Cook until smooth.

Note: Don't use aluminum utensils when making this recipe.

REFRIGERATOR PICKLES

7 cups sliced cucumbers
1 cup sliced onions
1 tablespoon pickling salt

Mix above and let stand for 1 hour. Then drain well, but do not rinse.

2 cups sugar
1 cup white vinegar
1 teaspoon celery seed
1 teaspoon mustard seed

Combine above and cook to boiling. Pour over cucumbers, mixing well. These will keep in refrigerator indefinitely.

GREEN TOMATO PIE

Green tomatoes
4 tablespoons vinegar
Butter
1-2 cups sugar
2 teaspoons cinnamon
Double pie crust

Peel and slice enough green tomatoes to mound up in the bottom crust. Sprinkle with the vinegar. Place pats of butter over the tomatoes. Mix the sugar with cinnamon and cover tomatoes before placing the top crust on the pie. Bake ten minutes in a hot oven. Reduce heat to 375 and bake another 40 minutes.

My Mother was "reminiscing":

"I've worn hand-me-downs all my life and usually was glad to get them--except when I was a young girl and had to wear castoffs from my cousin. She weighed 50 pounds more than I did and, besides, I thought she was nasty and overbearing!

When plans were made for the school picnic, she said, 'Don't have HER bring sandwiches. She'd bring homemade bread and stinky butter.' That comment was from someone who always gobbled my Mother's homemade bread. Her bread was delicious--made the old fashioned way where you make the yeast batter in the evening and set it overnight and add remaining flour the next morning."

After I read these thoughts of my Mom, I included a bread recipe that was similar to the one my Grandmother used. Find it on page 73.

DANDELION JELLY

Pick 1 quart dandelion flowers. Boil in 1 quart water, then strain. Add juice of two lemons. Cook half with one package powdered pectin and 4 cups sugar according to directions in the package.

LAMBSQUARTERS GREENS
Chenopodium Album

When Grandpa married Grandma he told her to fix him some dandelion greens. Grandma said "Ugh" but she fixed them. When Dad married Mom he said, "Let's have some lambsquarters greens." Mom said "Ugh" but fixed them, and they were great--tasted just like fresh green peas.

RECIPE

In early spring, pick at least a gallon of tender lambsquarters. Wash and put in a kettle with a small amount of water. Boil a short time until all are wilted. Serve with salt and butter.

MUSTARD PICKLES

1/2 cup dry mustard
1/2 cup salt
1 cup sugar
2 quarts vinegar
2 quarts water

Cut cucumbers in chunks and place in 8 quart jars. Pour cold brine over cucumbers. Seal. Will keep for 3 months.

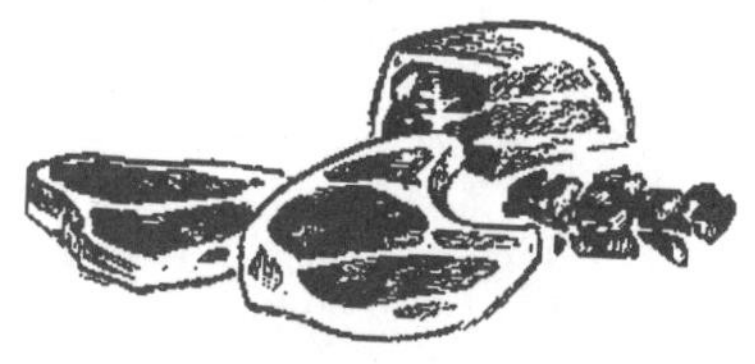

One lemon yields approximately 1/4 cup juice while an orange usually yields 1/3 cup juice.

WHIPPED CREAM KRUMKAKE

1 cup sugar
1/2 cup margarine
1/2 cup cream, whipped
3 eggs
1 1/4 cups flour

Cream sugar and margarine. Add cream and eggs and then the flour. Bake on a krumkake iron. Makes 4-5 dozen.

Use ice blocks in your punch bowl. Ice cubes melt too fast and will dilute the punch.

MORE RECIPES FROM THE GOOD OLD DAYS:

LOVE RECIPE

Take a cup of Kindness
Mix it well with Love
Add a lot of Patience
And Faith in God above
Sprinkle very generously
With Joy and Thanks
and Cheer
And you'll have lots of
"Angel Food"
To feast on all the year

Index

A Taste of Prairie Life

INDEX

MAIN DISHES

BEEF AND PORK:

CHICKEN AND FISH:

CASSEROLES:

SOUPS AND STEWS:

SOUPS AND STEWS, CONT.:

MISCELLANEOUS MAIN DISHES:

BREADS

BREADS AND QUICK BREADS:

BREADS AND QUICK BREADS, CONT.:

SALADS AND VEGETABLES

SALADS:

VEGETABLES:

VEGETABLES, CONT.:

DESSERTS

PIES:

CAKES:

COOKIES AND BARS:

COOKIES AND BARS, CONT.:

CANDY:

OTHER DESSERTS:

APPETIZERS AND BEVERAGES

APPETIZERS:

MISCELLANEOUS

THANK YOU!

A very special thanks goes out to my family, Jerry, Tracy, Travis, Mom, Dad, Hal and LeAnn, and to my friends who helped get this book to press! Thank you Dave for offering to distribute the book, Duane for the use of your equipment plus Kay, Linda and Delaine for your expertise, encouragement *and work!*

Prairie praises to all who shared their recipes, remedies and reminiscings with me, including:

Jerry, Tracy and Travis
Dorothy Vaad
Edith Werner
Alvin Werner
Pat Blum
SD Cattlewomen and
SD Cowbelles Red Beef
Cookbook
Mary Liz Schlotte
Edna Gunderson
Linda Den Beste
Ruth Blum
Mollie Vaad
Gertrude Harless
Annabell Homan
Brett Werner
Laura Reis
Mary Pat Fawcett
LeAnn Werner
Geneva Krois
Octavia Den Beste
Jeanne Holst
Hal Werner
Delaine Ellis
Stephanie Williams Roberts
Carol Boyd
Thunderstik Lodge

Efe Harless Williams
Sharon Weber
Bro. David Nagel
Father John Klingler
Brenda Allderdice
Jack Allderdice
Peggy Allderdice
Linda McFarland
Mary Haaland
Josephine Schwenke
T. Gwen Williams
Carol Shrake
Alice Olson
Cheryl Jordan
Dori Gunderson
Dixie Thompson
Marcia Blecha
Kay Andera
Shandra Thomas
Dina Brandt
Naoma Rossow
Terry Hogan
Mark Werner
Donna Dominiack
Agnes Ekstrum
Elva Von Eye
Ron Schara
Timothy Burrell

ORDER FORM

Please send __________copies of A Taste of Prairie Life, @ $12.95 each _________________, plus shipping and handling fee of $ 2.50 each_____________, **SD residents add 4% sales tax,

TOTAL__________________________

Name:____

Address:____

____

****

ORDER FORM

Please send __________copies of A Taste of Prairie Life, @ $12.95 each _________________, plus shipping and handling fee of $ 2.50 each_____________, **SD residents add 4% sales tax,

TOTAL__________________________

Name:____

Address:____

____

++

Make checks payable to Buffalo Grass Trading Co. If charging to your credit card, send card number, name on card and expiration date.

Gift card forms can be found on reverse side of order form.

NOTE: PRICE OF $12.95 PER COOKBOOK IS GUARANTEED THROUGH DECEMBER 1996.

GIFT CARD INFORMATION

Please send A Taste of Prairie Life cookbook to the following:

Name:____

Address:______________________________________

____

Message:

____

GIFT CARD INFORMATION

Please send A Taste of Prairie Life cookbook to the following:

Name:____

Address:______________________________________

____

Message:

____

GIFT CARD INFORMATION

Please send A Taste of Prairie Life cookbook to the following:

Name:____

Address:______________________________________

____

Message:

NOTES:

NOTES: